Courting The Wild Queen

Seán Pádraig O'Donoghue

Courting The Wild Queen

Seán Pádraig O'Donoghue

ISBN: 979-8-9852028-2-3

Layout and Production Editing: Rhyd Wildermuth

Copy Editing: Gwynevere Kipling

RITONA PRESS

an imprint of RITONA a.s.b.l

3 Rue de Wormeldange

Rodenbourg, Luxembourg

L-6995

View our catalogue and online journal at
ABeautifulResistance.org

Contents

for Mo Bhanríon Fiáin

Of Once and Future Worlds

There are those who say that this world is ending. They are not wrong. Perhaps it will be because we transformed ourselves into a culture whose values and perspectives and ways of living are so radically different from those of this civilization that they have more in common with the Otherworld than with the current iteration of this one. Maybe it will be because we failed to change ourselves, and thus change was forced upon us by war, famine, and climate disaster. Either way, life a generation from now will not resemble anything we now recognize.

This is nothing new.

Worlds die and are born every day. Every time a living being —a Cedar or a Salmon or a Bear or an Eagle—dies, an entire way that the universe experienced itself ceases to be. Every time a seed sprouts or a child is born, an entirely new way of being begins to emerge.

The end that is near is bigger than that. But this, too, is nothing new. Worlds have come and gone many times in the history of this species and this planet.

As the Earth's fever spikes, melting ice uncovers ancestral artifacts and desiccated fields reveal forgotten megaliths. Our ancestors are speaking to us through the fever dream, reminding us that there are other ways to live.

Our bodies, too, are awakening to the ancient memories they carry from the human and the other-than-human kin who went before us.

These bodies and these lives mirror the body and the life of the Earth.

In the wake of a season of burning forests, a virus rages through the human population, attacking our lungs and bringing us each and all either deeper into fever's delirium or to the point where the fever breaks and clarity returns.

We share a common fate and the common possibilities for healing, fulfillment, liberation, and flowering.

How do we navigate such times?

Albert Einstein is falsely rumored to have been the first to say that the problems we face will not be solved by the ways of thinking that created them. Whoever did say it first was insightful and wise.

We cannot imagine Once and Future Worlds solely with the knowledge and perspectives available to us from the dying culture we seek to replace. So, where do we turn for guidance?

Our ancestors knew that the world is alive and always speaking. They understood how to listen.

We were made to forget by a culture that can only accomplish the violence it has visited on our human and other-than-human kin by making us feel alien and alone until our bodies no longer feel the spinning iron core that is the beating heart of the Earth. But our bodies have the innate capacity to know her songs again.

Our souls have the Will to awaken and fully connect with Her and with ourselves. Myth and folklore, fragments of half-remembered practices and traditions, artifacts and monuments, and snatches of song hint at things we knew in other bodies and other lives. Poetry, ritual, rhythm, and dance open us. The beating of our hearts and the touch of the world on our senses invite us back into connection. Plants and animals, rivers and stones, wind and rain remind us of other ways to be in bodies on the Earth.

The poetry and prose of this book are an attempt to capture what the living world speaks to and through me. This is not a linear journey. Do not be alarmed if you feel a bit lost at times, just let the flow of the song at the heart of this text carry you awhile.

I invite you to read these words aloud, to find how they shift your heartbeat and your breath, how they feel on your tongue. I invite you to discover what words, what memories, what sensations, they awaken in you.

In the words of Robert Hunter, "if you get confused, listen to the music play."

A Note on Language and Gender

Gender is infinite in its expressions. The English language is not.

I wrestled a great deal with this conundrum when writing this book. It is my experience that when the wild and divine want to engage with us, they take on the forms we are most ready to engage. Some of this has to do with our interpretation of our perceptions and some of it with their intention.

Since so much in this book is raw and personal, I opted to describe the other-than-human beings with whom I shared this journey in the ways in which I experienced their presence. Their presence for me has often been gendered. It has felt most honest to me to portray them as such, even while understanding that my experience and my descriptions are limited by the ways in which this culture has shaped the limits of my imagination. When writing about history, I have preserved the gendered terms of the time of which I speak.

I invite readers whose experience of gender is very different from mine to re-imagine these encounters and descriptions and accounts in the ways that are right and true to you. I encourage you to write the books that will broaden the imaginations of people who have grown up in a culture wedded to limiting ideas of gender and sexuality that do not reflect the great wheel of life's reality in this world. May humanity one day understand the poles of duality are always reaching out to one another so we might be blessed by ever-changing diversity in so many variations.

A Note on Mythological Correctness

There are scholars of history and archaeology and anthropology and Gaelige literature whose work I love and admire. I am none of these things. I am a poet, an herbalist, and a priest.

Archaeology and anthropology, ethnography and literary scholarship can tell us much about the relationships the people of a particular time and place have or had with gods, animals, plants, mountains, rivers, stars, and oceans. But they do not offer the last word on the nature of our other-than-human kin.

While I reference and draw on old stories and ancestral ways, my writing ultimately arises from my own relationships with the beings of this world and the Otherworld.

The Bear King

There are moments when the world cracks open. Sometimes through those cracks you see the reflection of who you really are in the curved mirror of the original darkness that came before time and space, the darkness that had fallen in love and in lust with Herself, giving birth to all things. In a holy orgasmic birth cry that contained all the sounds that would ever echo through Her infinite body, She called forth our names, setting in motion the events that would arrange matter and energy into the form that writes these words and the forms that receive them.

As that sound condensed into matter, it became the hydrogen contained in the water of our bodies as well as the bodies of stars in whose furnace was forged the iron in our blood. Looking at the night sky, we see our starry kindred. But we forget that we are as ancient and as powerful as they are.

In the glaring electric light of the world into which we were born, it is hard to see and recognize such kin, let alone remember them.

When our lives break open, sometimes we fall down a well so deep that when we look up, we see stars at noon, and make out the constellations that remind us of our inner landscape, of all that we contain—and the world as we previously knew it is completely and utterly transformed.

I write from the bottom of one of those wells, following the stars that make the body of the Great Bear as they point toward Polaris, the bright star of the north that guides us through the dark vault of heaven. There we gather what was exiled and cast into the outer darkness by the coming of civilization and reintegrate it to ourselves, thus ultimately emerging back into the world in the fullness of who we are, aligned along the pole that the star marks.

I now write as a ritual of summoning myself, of calling myself in through the cracks in the world. And I write for all who also seek to emerge into this time and place in the fullness of who they are.

Like earthquakes, the events that shake and crack open our worlds tend to come in rhythmic pulsations, with tremors before the big quake and aftershocks that follow. They are kin to the orgasmic pulsations that gave birth to the universe. When they are tearing life apart, they require a particular focus and orientation to ride the waves to the point where pain transforms into ecstasy.

With Bealtaine approaching in 2016, I walked away from a beautiful life that no longer fit me. I left a job, a community, an island, and a country that had been home to me for four years during which I'd grown and shifted as much as I could in that time and space, just as I had in so many other places and times before.

My earliest memories are of feeling "a stranger in a strange land," afraid I would never find somewhere I belonged. I did not yet know that I was autistic—that my brain formed synapses in wild fractal patterns different from those of the people around me and experienced sensation and emotion without the filters most people have. All I knew was that everything about me felt out of place: my big Celtic body in a world that valued the slim and the swift, my strange manner of speaking and thinking, my fascination and fixation on ancient times and distant places and strange other worlds, my challenges in performing tasks according to the linear logic most people follow, my struggles with understanding and relating to how people around me were experiencing the world. Their confusion and frustration with my inability to accept the world around me "as it was" created a sense of alienation that metastasized into shame. I locked pain deep down inside me and turned the anger that rose from it against myself, not understanding that violence inwardly directed is still violent. I felt worthless and hopeless, and recklessly damaged and dishonored connections with people I loved.

Time and time again I had followed threads of synchronicity and possibility to places I had believed could become my true home, only to discover that they were, at best, temporary refuges. That pattern had repeated itself once more.

As I became once again uprooted, the shame and terror that had stalked me since childhood rose in me like a pair of wounded beasts, shaking me to the core, and I felt as though the ground was crumbling beneath me and the stars were falling from the sky.

As my world crashed around me, I turned to my gods and my ancestors. Every day, I went to the Hawthorn up the road, bringing offerings and calling to the tree, to my Irish ancestors, and to the Queen of Elphame in rudimentary broken Gaelige. I began to awaken to the genetic memory and the echo in my pulse created by life before the centuries of violence that cut us off from connection to our lands, our community, and the living world.

I took part in a sweat lodge and sat in the hottest seat, where I wept, shook, and prayed, and then washed myself with clear water from a cold stream when I emerged.

I felt free—for a little while. That night the shame and fear returned. I excoriated myself for going through catharsis after catharsis without ever experiencing lasting change.

The next morning, as I drove back to the land where the sweat lodge had been held, the radio belted out "She Moves in Mysterious Ways." The song ended and I switched off the radio, just as I turned onto a gravel road where I was met by a Black Bear.

The Bear and I watched each other for several minutes before the Bear ambled away and I continued up the road. When I arrived at the house, Meg, who had led the ceremony the day before, handed me a red cloth. I unwrapped it and found a Black Bear claw (...just in case I was about to attempt explaining away the Mystery that was unfolding.)

In the forests of North America's Pacific Northwest, where I lived at the time, Bear and Salmon are bringers of life—as they were in the lost Irish forests of my Paleolithic ancestors.

The oldest human artifact in Ireland is the carved jawbone of a Bear but by the time the Celts arrived in Ireland, Bears had been gone for hundreds of years. The Irish rainforest itself is now the trace of an echo of a memory.

On returning from the ocean to spawn and die, Salmon draw Bears to rivers and streams. Bears and Eagles drag fish carcasses into the forest where they enrich the topsoil.

In the Irish tradition, the Salmon is the oldest creature, and holds the wisdom of three worlds—the watery underworld it swims through, the airy heavens it leaps through, and the earth its body returns to. Whoever eats the body of the Salmon gains that wisdom.

Bears gorge on Salmon in autumn, and then retreat into their own dark underworld where their dreams are shaped by the mycorrhizal songs of the sleeping forest. When they stir in spring, they dig their medicine roots—plants like Osha and Angelica and Skunk Cabbage, which the herbalist Matthew Wood notes are "brown, furry, pungent, and oily" like Bears themselves, roots whose medicine stirs their blood and awakens their breath as they emerge from their winter slumber.

Wherever people and bears live in proximity, humans have traditionally followed the Bears' example: digging and decocting those same roots. They have also told stories of people who married those strange dark giants who rear up on two legs.

Bears are wild kin who walk between worlds, helping us remember who we are.

A bright spirit arrived in my life right about then, calling me forth and away from madness. Solar in her warmth and light, she called to me just as the scent of deep forest and dark waters about me called to her. By day, I was keeping it all together, teaching classes and tending patients. I spent April evenings that year wandering through the forest, singing fragments of *The Ballad of Tam Lin* and April nights listening to recordings of the ballad over and over again. I saw us both in the story but thought only of the woman pulling forbidden Roses who fell in love with a wild shade. I forgot the process by which she brought him into the human world.

Then he appeared in her arms
Like the Bear that never would tame.
She held him fast, not letting him go,
In case they would never meet again.

Then he appeared in her arms
Like the fire burning bald.
She held him fast, let him not go,
He was as iron could.

And he appeared in her arms
Like the adder and the snake.
She held him fast, let him not go,
He was her world's make.

And he appeared in her arms
Like to the Deer sae wild.
She held him fast. Let him not go
He's father o' her child.
And he appeared in her arms
Like to a silken string.
She held him fast, having him not depart,
Till she saw fair morning,

And he appeared in her arms
Like to a naked man
She held him fast, let him not go,
And with her he's gone home.

Nevertheless from Samhain until Midsummer, we lived that part of the tale.

Lenore Kandel wrote, "the divine is not separate from the beast." As a priest of the old gods I know that to be true. It is through the ecstasy of our animal self that we are able to experience our own infinity and divinity in ways that thought and language can never fully describe. But the judgments that our minds place on our animal selves imbue them with the shame, fear, and guilt which are fed life force every time we repeat those judgments, cursing our own bodies and the body of the world. We lock away the wild and in doing so, separate ourselves from the divine.

When the wild again awakens within us, at first it is like a caged beast breaking free that remembers its pain and its terror before it remembers its magnificence.

As my shame and fear of confusion overwhelmed me, I raged against myself, not knowing who I was, believing myself to be a monster that needed to be restrained or destroyed. I saw myself change from one terrifying form to another, rending the fabric of my own life.

She held me tight and feared me not, never forgetting who I was. But I could not remember and I would not look at the starry mirror for fear it would reveal the grotesquerie I believed myself to be.

I feared that if I permitted myself knowledge of the fullness of my desire, I would be predatory in the sense which a culture which does not know the ways Wolf and Orca imagines predators—not understanding the language and dance of consent and interdependence between hunter and hunted in the wild. I forgot that Her holy lust was the reason matter and energy born of the darkness arranged itself to become my personality. I conflated masculinity with violence and oppression, ceding its definition to the culture whose transfiguration I pray for.

In the tradition I embrace, we speak of the Peacock Lord who could send thunder and earthquakes through all the worlds with a single shake of his tail but is held still by the hand of his beloved Star Goddess, the Mother of All Things. I feared that if I allowed myself to embody power, I would tear my world apart, not trusting Her hand to hold me still when stillness was required and release me when the time came to shake the foundations of a civilization that threatened the survival of the world.

And so I engaged in the ultimate blasphemy that constitutes the rejection of the body that is Hers, the sex that is Her sacrament, the power that is the movement of Her love across space and time.

Gwydion (the late adopted spiritual son and initiate of Victor and Cora Anderson in the Feri tradition) started showing up at Samhain. I started leaving Cannabis offerings for him every Friday night, and soon he was a regular visitor. A herd of Deer would show up and I would know it was time for a spirit walk with Gwydion.

Gwydion Pendderwen was trained in the Craft beginning in his teenage years when Elon, the Andersons' son, brought Gwydion home with him. Victor and Cora had both grown up steeped in folk magic in the early part of the 20th century. They stirred what they learned from their forebears together with their own insights, encounters with gods and spirits, and past life memories to bring forward a magical tradition that was at once both ancient and new. Gwydion and Victor shared a birthday, many past lives, and a gift for poetry. Gwydion brought more Irish and Welsh elements into the cauldron of magic that Victor and Cora cooked.

Gwydion also brought some of his generation's irreverence and countercultural values concerning consciousness expanding plants, fungi, and chemicals, as well as sex and relationships. This sometimes generated friction with Victor and Cora, whose minds were usually quite open but who also valued the decorum of an earlier time. Gwydion was brilliant and sometimes rash, which worried Victor.

Gwydion was the great bard of his generation and his poetry, liturgy, and music often circled around the mythology of the Sacred King, who was sacrificed for the good of the land and the people. Some believe that his deep identification with that mythos played a role in his early death. This was part of what he came to warn me about. But there was another dimension as well.

Gwydion died in a car accident just after Samhain in 1982. He was 36 years old. One story I have heard is that Gwydion swerved to spare the life of a Deer in the road. He had a powerful relationship with the Stag as the embodiment of the sacred King, the kind of relationship that usually gives rise to a prohibition on killing the animal.

Not long before he died, he had shot a Deer in the garden. Gwydion was carrying a lot of regrets and spent his last day on earth visiting people he had once been close with, trying to make amends for ways he felt he had done them wrong.

What Gwydion then wanted me to understand was the mortal danger that guilt and shame create for a priest. Shame at its ultimate root is a belief that we don't have the right to continue to exist. Everything we feel becomes a prayer we make, a spell we cast. Those working with intense magic are running an especially strong current of power through our bodies, amplifying our prayers. When guilt and shame are sufficiently deep, they can become our own unconscious death prayers, especially if we also inhabit a myth that tells us that when we cease to bless the world, we must be sacrificed (a word that at its root means "made sacred.")

If we do not believe in our own sacredness, we court suffering and death in an effort to purge ourselves of what we believe makes us unworthy of the grace of divine love and passion.

There are particular dangers for priests socialized as men in a patriarchal culture who come into an intimate connection with the source of all life. Holding onto the identification with our culture's model of masculinity lends to either side of the coin of false pride: hubristic self-aggrandizement or abject self-annihilation. This warps the mirror of time and space in which we behold ourselves, just as God Herself did in the beginning and from which we conjure forth worlds, just as God Herself does now. That misperception can cause us to experience the infinite love of the Mother of All Things as rage or rejection and live our lives accordingly. The failure to address this kind of complex is a breach of the vow of love we have made to that Beloved Mother, and the sharp edges of a broken vow are a weapon we turn on ourselves. We can come to believe that only death can set things right.

Gwydion wanted to show me another way of taking up the path of the sacred King, of making my life an offering to the land and the people. Being an anarchist, I wasn't quite sure I wanted to engage kingly myths, and at least part of me just didn't want to die. Yet, something told me these objections were diversions from courting my own power and my own sovereignty and stepping into my real work.

The tradition and the culture were not my own but I was welcomed into the medicine ceremony with open arms, and there was a strange familiarity to the rhythms of the songs and the bitterness of the medicine. It was right around Imbolc, and I could feel the land beginning to generate life beneath the snow.

My ancestors had their own version of this ceremony, performed in caves and stone chambers with mushrooms and a goat skin drum, but only the slightest echoes of that tradition survive. After midnight, we were invited to go outside to drink water and greet any ancestors who desired an audience with us.

Gwydion showed up, of course, and asked me to pay deep attention to what was about to happen. When I returned to the tipi and drank the medicine, I had visions of a similar fire and a similar drum in a stone chamber, and a sacramental mushroom tea. The medicine was showing me the ways of my own ancestors a continent and an ocean away.

I heard a song, its rhythm and its intonation resonant with echoes of Indigenous North American music but its words a Gaelige and proto-Celtic creole:

> *"Se do beatha bhaille, Art- rí Dubh"*
> "Welcome home, Black Bear King"

It was the song for recalling the fullness of my being into this world.

When the sun rose and shone through the opening in the tipi, I had an image of the sun coming through an opening in the stone chamber, just as the light flowed from the darkness when, as Victor said, "Darkness lay with death and love was born. Love lay with darkness and death and light were born."

Another vision, another understanding of kingship thus began revealing itself to me that night. In the old stories, the King is wedded to the land and his sovereignty is a gift the land bestows and withdraws at will. This suggests a very different notion of sovereignty than that which tends to be bandied about in the dominant culture today.

People now tend to speak of sovereignty as being individual and personal—our right to control our own bodies and lives. But the individual rational actor is an invention of capitalism, a concept that severs our connections to land and community. In reality, our bodies and our minds are ecologies—communities of myriad beings coming together and giving rise to a more or less shared consciousness—and are completely interdependent with the humans and other-than-humans who share our landscape. Just as a god might be the mind that arises from a forest, a river, a planet or a cluster of galaxies, so too is each person's consciousness a collective consciousness born of the matter and energy that make up our beings.

To be sovereign is to be in alignment, to be self-possessed—which inherently means to be conscious of the ecological selves we are members of in the same way that our individual neurons are members of a brain, a nervous system, a neuroendocrine emergent self-regulating feedback loop, a human body, a family, a community, a species, an ecology, a landscape, a planet, a solar system, a galaxy, a universe, and the body of God Herself.

To live in the knowledge of all these levels of consciousness and being can be overwhelming and may make it difficult to do the work of an ordinary human life. Communities evolve in ways that allow some to focus on embodying and anchoring these truths.

During the embryonic development of a human, some stem cells evolve to specialize in signaling processes and become neurons. Some evolve to specialize in detoxification, thus become liver cells. Some become the cells of muscle fibers to move the body through the world.

In the organic emergence of culture from community and ecology and landscape, two figures emerged who are integral to the life of the community but separate from it. The Witch in the hut at the edge of the village holds its circumference, the boundary, like the membrane of a cell—the site of communication with the outside world which also defines what is within and what is without. This is the very act of mediating between them. The King holds the center, like the nucleus of the cell, the repository of the genetic information about the world from which it arose rewritten by the experience of the cellular body.

The Witch and the King both know that the center and the circumference are one.

Ecologies are webs of sex and death. The sacred King is the tree to which people tie their colored ribbons and weave them in the dance. But if the tree is not rooted in the land, then it will topple—so also, if disconnected from the land, the King falls.

The King's relationship with the land is sexual in its nature. The King feeds pleasure, devotion and adoration to the land, and the land feeds the King and the people with blossoms, fruit, seeds and the bodies of Deer and Salmon. As long as the King feeds the land with love and the lust for life with dedication, the King may live. When the King ceases to feed the land life force, the King's body must be buried beneath an ancient mound or thrown in the bog.

The King who has lived a good life is buried with his ancestors beneath the Hollow Hills, held in the arms of his Wild Lover as his body dissolves into Hers and he prepares to be born again among his people. The King who has betrayed the land and the people is thrown into the bog where his body is preserved by the tannins from the peat so he will not be born again soon. This was not a punishment but a balancing. This is the real meaning of the idea that the King's life is given to the land as a sacrifice—when a King's life is lived in a way that is a gift of love freely given to the land and the people, then that life is a joyous and sacred gift. When the King's life ceases to be a gift of love freely given, then his death is the one remaining gift he can offer.

This form of Sacred Kingship stayed alive in Ireland well into the medieval era. At the *feis*, a great festival at Samhain, the time of honoring the dead of the *túath* (tribe), the King would make love to a woman who, as priestess and as Sacred Queen, embodied the spirit of the land. The king, historian Michael Richter tells us, was regarded as the embodiment of the people and was responsible for the wellbeing of the *túath*. He was without physical defects and his beauty was praised by the poets.

The physical beauty and spiritual radiance of the King inspired a river of vitality to flow from the people into the body of the King, and the beauty and power of the Sacred Queen inspired him to feed back to the land through her body.

The great King Nuada of the Tuath Dé, the Tribe of the Gods, the Shining Ones who went North to learn the secrets of the world and rode a black wind home, famously lost his arm in battle, which cost him his kingship for a time. One skilled healer forged him an arm of silver that allowed him to become a great warrior again. But the people remembered his kingship fondly and longed for him to be whole again. A healer of even greater skill channeled their will and their desire into Nuada's body which allowed him to grow back his own arm to again become their King.[1]

1. One of his descendants, Mug Nuadat, known also as Eóghan Mór, would become the founder of the Eóghanact tribe from which my own Ó Donnchadha sept would emerge.

John Moriarty said that a king is a dream of a people. But what happens when the people themselves no longer honor the life of the land and the sacredness of beauty and true power? They dream the king into a nightmare.

Through its confusion about power and its loss of connection to the living world, our civilization turned sex and even love into a crime, making it the original shame. We could no longer see the truth of our erotic lives: we are part of God Herself, formed to make love to Herself in myriad forms. Our bodies are the land itself come into human form to raise energy in ecstasy to feed it. Sex is a part of our ecological function, and it is diminished when we see it is only an interaction between individuals, rather than as a flow within an ecology, and it is diminished further when we objectify ourselves and each other.

Just as with the castrated Fisher King whose land became a wasteland when he refused to either heal or die, we curse the world in the process. The destruction we visit on Her body, which stirs the wrath of Her consort, is the expression of the loss of our erotic relationship with the body of the world. It is exacerbated by our feeding sexual energy to our own and each other's egos rather than to our god-selves, the land, and to our people. The consequences of that failure are heaviest for those who have made vows to the land or to God Herself in courting their own power. Their self-cursing in turn curses the world and they are cursed in return, a recirculating spiritual infection that becomes fatal if allowed to run its full course without interruption.

I was shown that the King and his embodied human lover formed a smaller erotic ecology which, when fed with love and trust, could become a self-regulating and self-healing system, in turn ensuring the health of the land and of its people. Those lovers were like stars in a constellation—coming together they revealed something of each other's nature and something of a shared pattern of being that made the figure of a Bear or a drinking gourd or a starry plough. Each of which was the center of its own constellation.

The first kings were priests, not hereditary rulers. They were oracular figures who spoke the law they heard in the movement of water over stone and the sound of wind in the trees, from the depths of the cave and sacred well bringing the law up from the land, not authority figures who handed down their own fiats, imposing them on the land.

This remained true to a large extent in Ireland until England broke apart the Irish tribes in the 16th and 17th centuries. Medieval Irish kings, if not necessarily formally filling a priestly role, continued to serve largely as the ceremonial figure who embodied the will of the people and united them in purpose and focus rather than as a political ruler in the modern sense, Richter tells us:

> "According to the legal texts, he did not have any legislative power, as the law was complete, comprehensive and independent. He was not even responsible for the maintenance of law, as this was the responsibility of the people. Offences were settled through the pronouncement of the legal scholars and were avenged by the victim's clan by way of the blood feud or the imposition of compensation. The king instead defended the túath against enemies from outside. Within the kingdom, he presided over the people's assembly (*oenach*)..."

Our longing for meaning and connection in an age of alienation has spawned a global industry based on hiring strangers to dig in our DNA to discover the secrets of our ancestry. Yet, we ignore or dismiss our oldest oral traditions and folklore. We do not remember that the Great White Sow was one of the oldest symbols of the Goddess and by her milk she feeds both Poets and Heroes. We forget the Goddess of ten thousand breasts.

Traditionally, when the King no longer truly fed the people, his nipples were cut off and the royal body was thrown into the bog. In other parts of the world when the King could no longer sexually function with the representative of the Goddess, he was retired by sacrifice or stepped aside for another to ascend. Failure to perform one ecological function results in shifting into the performance of another. Sex and death are the currencies of wild sovereignty.

Art-rí Dubh, "Black Bear King." Some scholars believe that the name of King Arthur may be derived from the proto-Celtic word *art-* which is related to the Greek word arctos and means "Bear" (which in modern Irish is *béar*) and the Irish word *rí*, which we translate as "King" today, and is related to the Sanskrit *rig* which means "shining."

Art-rí is so close to the Irish *Ard-rí*, "high King," that the latter could have easily evolved from the former. If so, this would put the origin of sacred kingship in Ireland within either the late Paleolithic or early Neolithic era, when Bears still roamed the island and long before the Gentry went beneath the hollow hills to become the Daoine Sidhe, the People of the Mound.

Perhaps the mounds themselves were inspired by the caverns and hollows where Bears hibernated.

Dubh means "black" in Irish, as does the related suffix *du* in Welsh, showing up in the name of the *Clogwyn Du'r Arddu*, the stone beneath which a sleeper will become "mad, dead, or a poet," and also in the name of the god who opens the gates of death.

Black is the color of the north in old Irish traditions, the place where the Shining Ones had learned the secrets and magics of nature. It is the color of the womb and of the grave. It is the place of beginnings and the darkness beneath the Hollow Hills where the Old Ones sleep. Ancient Irish cosmology saw all things as having their origin in darkness from which light then flowed.

But why a Bear King?

Victor said that anything that is true is observable in nature. The Salmon mirrors one understanding of sacred kingship—expending all of its energy to swim upstream to and for sex and death to give life to a generation of Salmon as it spawns and gives life to the forest when it rots and dies.

The Stag reflects another dimension—shedding its antlered crown each year and growing one anew. Think of Robert Cochrane's cipher of "the Roebuck in the Thicket"—one of the Stag's mysteries is that in the battles of the rutting season, he is at once the hunter, the hunted, and the hunt.

The Bear King is something else, something older. The Bear goes into the underworld for a season and then returns. The Bear King pays the debt of death to the land not by forfeiting body or life, but by spending the dark months of the year dreaming deeply with the roots, the Bears, the land, and the stars turning in the cold winter sky. Three months out of the year, the Bear King returns to the womb of the land, which is also his grave as well as his cavern of initiation and the cauldron of rebirth, deeply listening in ritual and trance to what the land would have the people know.

As the light returns and life stirs in the land at Imbolc, he rises to walk in the world again, digging pungent roots whose scent stirs the waters and the blood within his lovers' bodies. While the sun burns longer than the night, he serves the land by walking among the people. In the dark months, he serves the people by lying with the land.

The Bear King is a psychopomp at the gate of death, ecstasy, and birth. He returns in these times to give death to a culture severed from the living world and already rotting on its uprooted vine, and to sing enchantment back into the world and sing the world back into enchantment.

And so, as the wheel of the year turns toward Samhain, I come around to understanding my ecological role in this time and place. As the darkness descends, I spend long nights by a fire that warms my bones and stirs their memory. Sometimes in the flames, I see a vision of a Wild Queen. In the wake of the Owl's call, I hear the tinkling of silver bells. When the Queen's Seven Sisters rise just before the morning sun, I will meet her beneath the Hawthorn.

The May Queen

"True Thomas lay on Huntlie bank,
A ferlie he spied wi' his ee,
And there he saw a lady bright,
Come riding down by the Eildon Tree.
Her shirt was o the grass-green silk,
Her mantle o the velvet fyne,
At ilka tett of her horse's mane
Hang fifty silver bells and nine."
—Thomas Rhymer (Child Ballad 37A)

In early May, the Hawthorn blooms as its Scorpionic scent of sex and death starts mingling with the Bealtaine air. It is here I come to bring offerings of honey and whiskey to the Queen of Elphame, praying:

A Bhanríon na Bealtaine,
A Bhanríon na coil

A Bhanríon cumhra
A Bhanríon bláthú

A Bhanríon dearg
A Bh anríon glas

A Bhanríon ban
A Bhanríon dubh

A Bhanríon ionúin
A Bhanríon fiáin

Is mise do leannán fiáin
Is mise d'fhile fiáin
Is mise do rí fiáin[2]

It was at the edge of this same field that a dear companion and I found most of the skeleton of an Elk, dragged into the wash by a Cougar, and picked clean by Coyotes and Ravens a little before Imbolc two years ago; a reminder that in Winter, the May Queen becomes the Bone Mother, the Cailleach. Just after Imbolc, the heady seductive perfume of the Cottonwood buds brought the reminder that spring's sweetness would soon return, even though the snow was still deep upon the ground. Now, Spring has arrived and the Hawthorn blooms.

Sex and death, always inseparable, are marked by a biochemical cipher in the strange musky scent of the Hawthorn flower. Most flowering plants release light hydrocarbon molecules, monoterpenes, sesquiterpenes, and simple phenols that signal our bodies to move into a relaxed and open state of

2. I am not fluent in Gaelige; I have just enough of the language for my heart's prayers to express themselves as Gaelige now and then. I cannot vouch for the grammatical or orthographic correctness of any of the Gaelige in this strange little tome.

embodied presence and feelings of deep connection with the living things around us.

The Hawthorn flower releases an animal-like scent—a light molecule that incorporates a nitrogen atom into a carbon ring, becoming an alkaloid and an amine at that, like our own neurotransmitters. This particular amine, triethylamine, is what gives human sexual fluids part of their characteristic scent, and it is also released when flesh decays. *La petite mort et la grande mort.*

When we smell animal scents, our nervous systems become aroused—the valence of that arousal can move in different directions, however. Early in its blossoming, the Hawthorn releases a bouquet of more typical floral scents along with the triethylamine. The relaxation of tension brought on by the terpenes and phenols tilt the body's response to the arousal brought on by the musky alkaloid in an erotic direction, just as our lovers' pheromones mingle with triethylamine in their sexual fluids, giving meaning and context to our arousal.

In Ireland and Scotland alike, Bealtaine began when the Hawthorn first bloomed, a festival of ecstasy that also marked a time when the shining ones who dwelt beneath the hollow hills would walk among humans. Perhaps the lusty embodiment that the scent of Hawthorn evoked in the people made them more like their wilder kindred who had left this world at the advent of civilization. The presence of the wild and the divine being transgressive, the proximity of the Otherworld made Bealtaine, like Samhain, in some ways inherently a festival of misrule.

The Romans never conquered Ireland, and were driven back from Scotland by fearsome warriors, women and men fighting side by side. They were convinced that this was not just a battle against people but also against the ancient Gods of the land itself.

Their successors, the Christianized people of Britain who later partially colonized Ireland in the 12th century, held that their one God was all powerful but they hedged their bets. Partly to win the allegiance of the people and partly to avoid direct conflict with powerful spirits that might or might not exist, they allowed some of the old festivals to continue, transmuted at least on the surface, into the feast days of saints.

Bealtaine was a festival of unruly bodies, which Catholicism attempted to co-opt into a Marian feast, not understanding that for people steeped in an animist experience, albeit one with a syncretic Christian overlay, the Mother of God would be a profoundly sexual figure.

Mary, of course is, known among those who love her as Our Lady. She would have been understood by many as a more universal version of the sovereignty goddesses who were the living spirit of the land where she dwelled. She and sainted women received devotions at the same holy wells where people had always honored those spirits.

Lady is also the literal meaning of the name of the Norse Goddess Freyja, who came in small ways to Ireland and in more pronounced ways to Scotland and parts of England with Viking raiders and settlers. The Queen of Elphame is another name of Freyja well known in Scotland and used interchangeably with that of the bright Faerie Queen. Freyja is a warrior and a great beauty, a goddess of fertility and pleasure and victory, and the one who taught magic to her priestesses, the volva, and to Odin, the great King who sacrificed himself to himself for the sake of knowledge. Once Christianity was compulsory, it was only logical that much of her veneration would be translated into devotion to Mary.

The Protestants, whose theology and religious praxis co-arose with capitalism, understood full well the challenges that rural seasonal festivals posed to convincing people to be industrious. These festivals were inconsistent with the idea that God wanted people to transform His creation into merchandise.

In England, a new moneyed class that profited from Spain's repaying its debts to Britain with looted gold from the Americas demanded land, and the Crown and Parliament responded with the policy of "enclosure" which divided and privatized land people had farmed in common since the emergence of agriculture in Britain. Unable to pay rent or taxes, families were uprooted and fled to the cities where they would become the workforce of the developing industrial economy or across the sea to America where they took part in the forced displacement of other people from their ancestral homes.

Men's bodies became engines of production. Women, who had held strong positions in the family and the community when people worked the land in common, became a source of unpaid domestic labor and their bodies became engines of reproduction. Many women who refused to comply and conform were charged with witchcraft, then tortured and executed during these times. (See Silvia Federici's *Caliban and the Witch*).

It is worth noting that the armed resistance to the enclosures in England may have appealed for aid to the faerie realm with their mythical leader, whose face was never seen as General Ludd, possibly being an iteration of the Brythonic faerie King, Llud, as Rhyd Wildermuth and others have suggested. Llud was likely a Welsh and Pictish variant of the Irish Faerie King Nuada, a venerated ancestor who traveled with Irish people of the Eóghanacht tribe who ruled over parts of those regions well into the 8th century. And like an ancient King, General Ludd was indeed a defender of the land and the embodiment of the will of the people.

Derisive propaganda depicted Ned Ludd as wearing a dress with one shoe off and one shoe on. On one level, this was a reference to the raucous festivals of misrule that had once been the pressure valve keeping British society from exploding, but now were banned by the emerging Puritan order. (The original "War on Christmas" was waged by fundamentalists who wanted to put an end to bawdy merrymaking in the streets of London and keep it from the newly laid streets of Boston). He was the once Holy Fool who no longer had a place in the dour and orderly world of the dawn of capitalism.

On another level, it was a mockery of a dying rural culture. Men were seen as feminized if they listened to the women who kept alive old wisdom and old rites, the "Old Wives" who told tales filled with the echoes of ancient wisdom and practical knowledge of the land. To break people's ties to the land, it was necessary to criminalize and marginalize those who kept those ties alive—the midwives and healers. England's witch persecutions were an attempt to eradicate a culture. The Luddites were the men who still honored women's wisdom and still knew there were spirits alive in the land. They fought and died to defend their families' way of life.

Up through the 18th century, rural political resistance in England maintained a bawdy and distinctly animist character and clothed itself in symbols of the old May rites of the Celtic Pictish culture that preceded the coming of the Anglo-Saxons, the Romans, and the Normans and continued to survive in hidden ways in the countryside. British historian E.P. Thompson writes that while by the late 18th century, revolutionary politics took on forms easily recognizable to us,

> "as we move backward from 1760 we enter a world of theatrical symbolism which is more difficult to interpret:...It is a language of ribbons, of bonfires, of oaths and of the refusal of oaths, of toasts, of seditious riddles and ancient prophecies, of oak leaves and of maypoles, of ballads with a political double-entendre, even of airs whistled in the streets."

Within a generation, those Faerie Kings and Faerie Queens to whom the poor had looked for defense were reduced to quaint and dainty images of winged creatures on porcelain teacups.

Yet, at the same time, with the rural rebellions at home safely crushed, English society became willing to tolerate the eccentricity of the Romantics who sought to reconnect with the living land and with the legends of great Kings like Arthur and seductive Otherworld Queens. The spiritual descendants of the Romantics continued, launching a great occult renaissance.

Two centuries after the Luddites, in 1994 on the other side of the Atlantic in southern Mexico, another animist people resisting the enclosure of communal lands, the Mayans of Chiapas, would also take part in an armed uprising whose primary public voice was that of a masked (sub)commander Marcos, whose words broke down capitalist materialist logic with a combination of Mayan tradition, a bit of Marxist analysis, sometimes bawdy humor, and a touch of magical realism, whose words were disseminated through the internet. At one point, the Mexican government spread rumors that Sub-comandante Marcos was gay, hoping to discredit him. Marcos replied:

> "Marcos is gay in San Francisco, black in South Africa, an Asian in Europe, a Chicano in San Ysidro, an anarchist in Spain, a Palestinian in Israel, a Mayan Indian in the streets of San Cristobal, a Jew in Germany, a Gypsy in Poland, a Mohawk in Quebec, a pacifist in Bosnia, a single woman on the Metro at 10pm, a peasant without land, a gang member in the slums, an unemployed worker, an unhappy student and, of course, a Zapatista in the mountains."

The spirit of resistance shapeshifts across time and space, acting in ways not always understood by the people whose bodies it moves through.

It may be a mere synchronicity that International Worker's Day, commemorating the murder of eight anarchists by the state in Chicago in 1886, coincides with Bealtaine. Perhaps it is not a mistake that the forces that seek to disrupt the commodification of human bodies would end up being drawn to celebrate and assert liberation during the season when the Queen of Elphame is stirring the world into a life-affirming erotic awakening that resists all systems and modes of control. Nor is it a mistake, perhaps, that the festival of ecstasy would be overlaid with a festival to honor the revolutionary dead.

As the Hawthorn passes the peak of its bloom, the floral aspects of its scent fall away and leave us with just that musky alkaloid which, on its own, begins to smell putrid. Decaying bodies don't produce pheromones, and dying flowers produce fewer aromatic compounds, causing us to associate the scent of triethylamine on its own with dead and dying things.

The May Queen has a dark twin, the Cailleach Béara. She is stone and earth, older than the hills. She rules the dark of the year. Some say she is the bride of Manannán, great god of the sea waiting for him to return from beyond the waves.

Cailleach is the Cailleach Béara. She is stone and earth, older than the hills. She rules the often translated into English as "hag," a word whose modern connotations are bound up with our fear of the darkness and of the grave, which is also the darkness of the earth and the darkness of deep waters and the darkness of the womb.

When I see her, I see the color of moonlight and granite and driven snow. She smells of Hawthorn and Datura in flower and of Apples frozen halfway through fermentation. Her beauty is no less seductive that that of her twin.

In old stories, a man encounters a hag along the road who asks him to kiss her. The kiss blesses and transforms them both, and she becomes beautiful to him. With that blessing, the way opens for him to become the Sacred King who gives life to the land.

Who scorns the kiss is cursed.

The Cailleach's bright twin, he May Queen, comes in a flurry of white blossoms, smelling of sunlight and Wild Ginger. To paraphrase Rumi, "The price of her kiss is your life."

Whoever reads her kiss as a kiss of death does not understand the price. You will not die in that moment of bliss but like Oengus Óg, upon seeing the vision of Caer in the flames of the fire where he cooked the silver Trout, you will wander the worlds, following her scent on the wind. Or perhaps she will take you then and there.

Her kiss stirs something in your blood. Concrete and fluorescent lights become intolerable. The scent of Cottonwood, the call of the Raven, the song of the Wood Thrush, the flow of mountain streams will drive you to ecstasies you can barely conceal. You will seethe at the sight of fences that sunder the land.

You will forsake all lovers whose language is not touched by the music of her silver bells.

You will never be the same.

> "Light down, light down now, True Thomas,
> And lean your head upon my knee.
> Abide and rest a little space,
> And I will shew you ferlies three."
> —Thomas Rhymer (Child Ballad 37A)

Even then, She will still offer you a choice—or at least the illusion of one. You could call it all a demonic vision, return to the church, repent, and live a life of celibacy and asceticism. Or you could throw yourself into the arms of every lover you find, chasing the echo of the pleasure of her kiss, only to find that no sweetness or debauchery can match the briefest brush of her lips on yours unless the lover be one of Her Hidden Children, come to remind you who you are.

Or you could go with her. That path is the most perilous of all —and the only one that will set you free. She offers the choice in all sincerity but there was never any possibility that you would choose to be anywhere but by Her side.

In the ballad of Thomas Rhymer, as her human lover lays his head upon her knee, the Queen shows him three roads, stating:

> 'O see ye not yon narrow road,
> So thick beset with thorns and briers?
> That is the path of righteousness,
> Tho after it but few enquires.
> —Thomas Rhymer (Child Ballad 37A)

Some Christianized people accuse the People of the Mound and their Queen of using language to deceive—but it is Christian civilization which has justified cruelty in the name of love.

Righteousness presumes a single truth and a single correct response to that truth. It begins with an image of perfection against which we measure ourselves and a narrowing path toward its attainment. That path is lined with the thorns and briers of our own judgment that cut into our flesh if we stray, as inevitably we do. When we feel the first cut of thorn into flesh, we begin to dissociate, no longer trusting our bodies, and seeking instead the abstract maps in the left frontal cortices of our brains to lead us. And they lead us into the tangle of thorns again and again, because none of those maps resemble anything akin to the fluid realities of the living world.

The thorn is also the ward that protects the Otherworld from the incursion of this particular form of madness. The lone

Hawthorn stands atop the Hollow Hill barring the entry of those who would bring their cruel morality. Victor Anderson described their ways as "kinder...and less civilized." Those who dwell beneath have seen the iron chains that we place around our own hearts, the desires become the iron sword by which we impose our visions of righteousness on each other, and the iron plough with which we impose our straight-rowed monocrop vision on the body of the Earth.

It is common in our culture, when reflecting on the atrocities of the past few millennia, to ask how people could be so devoid of morality as to commit genocide and ecocide over and over again—however, the problem is not a lack of morality, but an excess of moral rigidity and moral fervor.

The violence inspired by the vision of righteousness inevitably turns outward. Whether we call them heretics or degenerates or counterrevolutionaries, those who refuse to conform to our concept of righteousness are soon defined as unworthy of living in the world that we are perfecting. The prison, the execution chamber, the guillotine, the gulag, and the concentration camp are the inevitable manifestations of ideologies of righteousness. The school, the psychiatric ward, and the mandatory rehabilitation program are the velvet gloves that liberalism threatens to slip off the iron fist of the state if people don't show adequate commitment to their own "improvement."

Righteousness shapes our dominant paradigm of justice, and social justice movements that fail to examine and question the nature of that paradigm quickly end up replicating it, seeking to identify and punish those whose language or concepts fail to conform to their own emergent orthodoxy. The threat of ostracism is a threat of social death that forces compliance. Corporations and the state learn that they can depend on their erstwhile opponents to distract and disable each other.

A handful of brazen individualists escape both fates and find their way onto the second road.

> 'And see not ye that braid road,
> That lies across that lily leaven?
> That is the path of wickedness,
> Though some call it the road to heaven.
> —Thomas Rhymer (Child Ballad 37A)

Every dominant term generates its inverse. Unsurprisingly, for many, the rejection of righteousness begins and ends with inverting its morality, resulting in an opposite form of enslavement—enslavement not by discipline but by unchecked insatiable appetites.

The conscious embrace of wickedness, the formula of reversal that breaks taboos for the sake of unlocking the power dammed up behind them, brings at best an incomplete liberation. If the erstwhile adept or the mundane freedom fighter is unprepared to engage and focus the power liberated, the magician can become its slave and the freedom fighter the new slaver.

The fact that cultural taboos around violence and sexuality are deeply oppressive does not mean that shattering all boundaries will set you free. There is a difference between the rigid limits of repression and the fluid, negotiated boundaries that evolve in living conversation. In a culture that has rejected the wild, we miss the fact that the wild has its own etiquette of consent.

If the road of righteousness is the road of abstraction, the road of wickedness is the road of objectification. Like the road of righteousness, it begins with cutting you off from the felt sense of connection with the living world, but it plays out more viscerally. As Victor Anderson said: "Harm comes from the root of the act. Is it reinforcing the shade and shadow of some awful event or is it truly a healing?"

The embrace of wickedness need not be conscious. It can be the result of trauma that cuts off our awareness of connection. When we believe that our world is unsafe and that we have to fend for ourselves, we come under the influence of norepinephrine and adrenaline, two of the hormones and neurotransmitters that narrow our focus to the single goal of survival at all costs. We constrict our muscles, our blood vessels, and our focus.

When the threatening situations we experience remain unresolved, as most of the stressful situations in contemporary life do, we remain constricted. The perceptual changes induced by constriction make it difficult to see anything outside the threat we perceive. We come under the influence of the hormone cortisol. Released by the adrenal cortex, cortisol serves to keep us in a position to respond to danger when an immediate threat has passed but we are not entirely safe yet. It acts to elevate our blood sugar so more energy will be quickly available to our muscles, to dampen the inflammatory responses brought on by the adrenaline and norepinephrine response we had to the initial threat, to favor the storage of excess energy as fat over the construction of muscle—and to make us more afraid of and prone to perceive immediate, cataclysmic threats in the world around us while also diminishing our cognitive capacities.

It is a set of responses that evolved to protect us from immediate, passing threats.

But what if the threat is hunger or imminent homelessness or misjudging one of the capricious moods of a fiery tempered boss—something that doesn't go away? Then the very constriction that serves to protect you by making you ready to fight or run or freeze may make it difficult for you to perceive the help and support available to you. You can become addicted to the accompanying biochemical cascade.

You might become so focused on surviving that you aren't able to respond or even pick up on the solidarity extended to you by allies. You might miss the voices of the ancestors whispering to you in your dreams or in the wind blowing through the Firs or the omens that may come by birds on the wing or the Bear in the wood letting you know that you are not alone. Worse still, the impact of your actions (or inaction) on the Firs, the animals, and your fellow humans will become invisible or irrelevant to you. But there is a path away from the brutalities of fear and wickedness.

> "And see not ye that bonny road,
> That winds about the fernie brae?
> That is the road to fair Efland,
> Where thou and I this night maun gae"
> —Thomas Rhymer (Child Ballad 37A)

Her kiss awakens the memory of another way of being, something you know in your bones and your blood—and your heart. Your body remembers the path that winds around the fernie brae, the road to Elfland.

The Irish call the people of that other realm the Daoine Sidhe—the people of the mound. They were the ones who found the civilization brought by Bronze Age navigators from Spain too cruel, and retreated to the Otherworld, the dark watery realm from which all rivers flow. They are identified with the animist ancestors of the Gaelige-speaking peoples of Ireland and Scotland. Victor Anderson said that their ways were kinder—and less civilized.

It was civilization that they fled in their return to the source of the wild waters. Echoing and invoking Henry David Thoreau's observation that "Nature is a prairie for outlaws."

Herbalist Stephen Harrod Buhner writes:

> "The word 'civilized' comes from the Latin 'civilis,' meaning under law, orderly. ... Civilis itself comes from the older Latin word 'civis,' meaning, 'someone who lives in a city, a citizen.' Those who go into wilderness, into Nature that has not been tamed, are no longer under (arbitrary) human law, but under the all-encompassing, inevitable law of Nature. They go out from under human law. They are no longer citizens, they are not orderly, they are not civilized—they are outlaws."

Civilization tells us that it exists to keep us from destroying each other and it defines the wild as a place of unbridled violence, "red in tooth and claw," to justify its own unrelenting, highly organized violence. The chaotic violence that arises from the trauma caused by structural violence is shown as proof of the need to maintain a rigid order.

We call those who inflict pain on others in unsanctioned ways "beasts" and "predators"—in a language that could only arise from a culture that has all but eradicated actual predators from most of their historic range, and so has no lived experience of the wild etiquette of consent that plays out between predator and prey. Biologists observing the interaction between Wolves and Moose on an island in Michigan observed what traditional hunters around the world already knew. There is a pause when the hunter and the hunted meet that allows for a subtle, embodied communication. Sometimes a Moose will offer itself up to the Wolf without a struggle. Sometimes a Moose will stare a Wolf down or defend itself, and the Wolf will walk away. Sometimes the Moose will turn and run, an invitation to chase. But only a sick and isolated Wolf will go on a rampage.

Wolves and Moose are not taught codes of behavior. Nor do they depend on any outside authority to enforce the terms of their unspoken agreement. Everything is communicated through their embodied experience of each other's presence.

Buhner points out that we humans have the same capacity to directly perceive the ways in which other living beings are experiencing us. He writes of the heart as an organ of perception that picks up on subtle fluctuations in electromagnetic fields, sending information about the same changes via the vagus nerve to the amygdala and to the right frontal cortex of the brain where we interpret it as emotion. This kind of direct communication of experience allows us to base our choices on a direct emotional empathy rather than on an abstracted set of rules and guidelines. Our capacity to engage that empathy grows the more we allow our awareness to shift to focus on our own embodied presence in each moment.

The trouble with such empathy is that it refuses to honor the rules of etiquette that guide civilization's preferred form of cognitive empathy which is marked and tested by the ability to correctly guess the internal experience and the desired response of another person by thinking about the situation and running it through the rubric of the normative experiences and responses of the majority population. More subversively, this wild type of empathy refuses to honor the rules set for whom or what we may empathize with and whose experiences should matter to us most. You are supposed to care more about the wellbeing of your family members than about the wellbeing of the man sleeping in the doorway of the bank, more about the death of an American soldier in a helicopter crash than about the deaths of twenty Yemeni civilians in a drone strike on a wedding party. And you are not supposed to empathize at all with trees or stones or rivers or stars. All those rules and categories break down when we bypass abstraction and go to a place of directly experiencing the presence of other beings.

In *The Function of the Orgasm*, Wilhelm Reich[2] wrote:

> "Today very few people know that morality was once regarded as a phylogenetically, indeed supernaturally derived instinct. This was said in all seriousness and with great dignity."

Reich saw civilization, and the sublimation of libido which Freud defined as its basis, as responsible for the suppression of this instinct. Alienation from our own bodies and from the experiences of other living, feeling beings is achieved through and reinforced through a body armoring, and the unconscious habit of holding tension in the muscles that create structural changes in the fascia. Reich observed that:

> "The character structure of modern man, who reproduces a six-thousand-year-old patriarchal authoritarian culture is typified by characterological armoring against his inner nature and against the social misery which surrounds him. This characterological armoring of the character is the basis of isolation, indigence, craving for authority, fear of responsibility, mystic longing, sexual misery, and neurotically impotent rebelliousness."

That armor is broken open through pleasure. The Queen's kiss has the power to liberate us and to restore our innate, wild empathy, the instinct that guides us in living in our reciprocal relationship with the human and other-than-human members of our ecological communities by bringing us into a radically embodied presence.

3. Wilhelm Reich was a great psychologist, scientist, and cultural critic. He was Freud's star pupil who became the *bête noire* of psychoanalysis when he took the position that the libido needs to be liberated in order to allow humans to be fully free and alive. He identified the libido with a form of energy present everywhere and in all things called orgone. He was one of the first to see the true nature of fascism, and spoke out against its rise, escaping Europe on the last boat out of Norway before the Nazis took over. He taught in New York for a time, and then moved to Maine where he devoted his life to learning to use orgone first for healing and then as an energy source, and a means of changing the weather. He was falsely accused of making unsubstantiated medical claims, and his books were burned by the FDA in the largest book burning in U.S. history. He refused to comply with a court order to stop his work and was arrested and died in prison. His tomb is on the hill that overlooks the cove where I kayak among the Loons.

True empathy is a function not of the socialized human talking aspect of the self but of our wild self which experiences the world through sensation and emotion.

It is significant that Thomas is instructed not to speak while in Elfland. Just before they wade across a river that contains all the blood spilled by the wicked and the righteous of the world, the Queen tells Thomas:

> 'But, Thomas, ye maun hold your tongue,
> Whatever ye may hear or see,
> For, if you speak word in Elflyn land,
> Ye'll neer get back to your ain countrie.'
> —Thomas Rhymer (Child Ballad 37A)

The language of civilization is worse than useless when navigating Otherworld landscapes or learning the ways of Faerie. Naming and categorizing things and attempting to place them within existing frameworks of understanding shifts us into the realm of the abstract. Being wilder, Faerie is a realm of emotion and sensation, a realm whose logic is the logic of myth and poetry and, well, faerie tale rather than the transactional language of a culture full of people separated from their own bodies and the body of the land.

Poetry is the primary instance where spoken and written language begin to reflect the experience of the wild self. Poetry is the result of the talking self-moving in rhythm with the wild self, while the wild self makes love to the part of us that knows our own infinity and divinity. Direct knowledge of our infinity and divinity would shatter the talking self. Poetry is the way we avoid madness or death when integrating the experience of the sublime or the horrific.

Poetry seeks to orient us in a universe of feeling. Perhaps this is why the Queen chose a poet to seduce. Irish philosopher John Moriarty touched on this when speaking of the nature of language in a Gaelige-speaking animist culture. He wrote:

> "To learn to speak is to learn to say, 'our river has its source in an Otherworld well,' and anything we say about the hills and anything we say about the stars is a way of saying 'A Hazel grows over the Otherworld well in which our river has its source.'"

In lectures and workshops, Moriarty contrasted this way of engaging language from the ways in which we use language to commodify the world and to negotiate trade. This is why indigenous languages are often the first aspect of a culture that colonizers try to eradicate.

Having spent seven years in Elfland, Thomas finds that his relationship with language has shifted. The Queen makes that change permanent by giving him the taste of an Apple from her world, a gift he protests but cannot refuse:

> "'Take this for thy wages, True Thomas,
> It will give the tongue that can never lie.'
> 'My tongue is mine ain,' True Thomas said;
> 'A gudely gift ye wad gie to me!
> I neither dought to buy nor sell,
> At fair or tryst where I may be.
> 'I dought neither speak to prince or peer,
> Nor ask of grace from fair ladye:'
> 'Now hold thy peace,' the lady said,
> 'For as I say, so must it be.'"
> —Thomas Rhymer (Child Ballad 37A)

Having eaten Otherworld Fruit, Thomas experiences a permanent fall from social grace, mirroring the separation of Eve and Adam from the love of a certain desert god who demands absolute obedience and frequently proclaims His jealousy.

This would be a good time to tell you that if you have not yet caught the Queen's scent on the wind or felt the ghost of the knowledge of the taste of her kiss, it is not quite too late to turn back. Proceed at your own peril.

Read this aloud, and you will begin to taste the wild. Buhner warns:

> "If we eat the wild, it begins to work inside us, altering us, changing us. Soon, if we eat too much, we will no longer fit the suit that has been made for us. Our hair will begin to grow long and ragged. Our gait and how we hold our body will change. A wild light begins to gleam in our eyes. Our words start to sound strange, nonlinear, emotional. Unpractical. Poetic."

When I first read those words, a few months after first encountering the Ballad of Thomas the Rhymer, I thought they were a metaphor. Now I am a wild-eyed, wild-haired poet whose every waking and sleeping breath carry the memory of the taste of the kiss of one who smelled of sunlight and Wild Ginger beneath a tree in May. The next kiss will be the kiss of my unmaking.

The Bone Mother's Cauldron

At Samhain, my Wild Queen comes dressed in white. The Hunter rises in the night sky and rides across the Milky Way and the Bears sleep beneath the earth, listening to the dream songs of the trees. All October, Coyote bones and Datura blossoms bedecked her altar. Now she beckons me out beneath the stars and bids me set the dry blooms petals aflame. Their scent is seductive like the Hawthorn but carries none of its warmth. Its shimmer is not the shimmer of sunlight on water but the shimmer of moonlight on snow. Narcotic in the crisp night air.

Forgetting the intoxication the smoke will bring, and the dangers of poisoning from inhaling too much, I bend over the burning flowers and breathe deeply.

I feel the Wild Queen at once as close as my breath and spread out across the whole night sky.

Her lips are as smooth as flower petals and as cold as the space between stars. Time slows. Frost spreads in fractal patterns across the ground. I feel a strange, frozen bliss moving through my body in the same way. I am sinking into darkness, into the silence between my heartbeats, the stillness between my breaths.

Then there is something at my root so cold that it burns, and the sensation rises up my spine. She whispers in my ear, "Not yet, my darling, not yet, but still, you will pass through the house of the dead, though you are not among them."

Through vespertine
tunnels at the center
of the flower

you follow the scent
into a dark hovel
where a wild haired woman
stirs fresh petals
into a cauldron
filled with your bones.

Drink it,
and you will know
what the Apple tree knows
when she drifts into winter slumber,
drunk on the fermentation
of her own rotting fruit

whose decay will feed
the seeds in springtime

and become the perfume
of the blossom before summer:

The lines are thin
between birth and death,
between kill and cure,
between ecstasy and terror.

What shimmers
in the twilight
and stirs desire

takes its life from the darkness,
where all knowing,
all healing
begins
and ends.

It is fashionable these days to undergo shamanic dismemberment over the course of a ninety-minute drum journey or a weekend workshop. Such cheap grace is worth exactly the price that is paid.

My Wild Queen will have none of that. Her desire is not to exact suffering or torment or penance. Blood sacrifice is the way of the false gods of civilization, not of those who came before.

She only desires that her lovers die to the culture that is killing the living world and allow something of lost worlds and lost peoples that has slept within our blood and the blood of two hundred generations before us to awaken. We have believed the personae we crafted to survive in "The World as It Is" to be an expression of our true selves. But no matter how radical that expression might be, it is still shaped by the assumptions and agenda of a culture that will not voluntarily expand to make room for the heralds and the vanguard of the Once and Future World that will replace it.

She will not deal the death blow herself. She loves Her Beloveds too much for that. But the price of Her first kiss is your Life. In that kiss, something that has slept beneath the surface awakens in you. It will not be fed by white bread and lab-grown meat substitutes.

We all know what happens when you come back from the wilderness with the taste of her lips on yours and a fire burning in your head that blazes green through your eyes and a heart that contains worlds. At first, the crowd will hunger to know what it is you tasted that gives you such an insatiable desire for the Wild and the Divine. When they brush against you, you will feel their pull.

They will make a road for you. They will lay down branches on your path. They will seem to want to follow you into the new and ancient world whose gates are opening in front of you. But the Wild and the Divine are inherently transgressive, and eventually you will transgress. You'll make a ruckus at the bank. Despite your lack of certification from the Reiki Alliance, people will say that your touch healed them... but it felt strange, there was something alive and green and pulsing in it that was not the white light of Ascended Masters and Heavenly Hosts.

Or, like me, you may have already had strange life stirring within you before She kissed you. But you might not have known the power of what moved through you. You welcomed some from the crowd in close who were not prepared to experience it. You were not prepared either. The life She would waken fully with Her kiss was already flowing through you like a wild spring from an Otherworld well, but it flowed through soil polluted by fear and shame and through brackish swamps of festering unshed tears, and it came out carrying their scent and taste. People got scared. People got hurt. You did not understand how and why until it was too late.

In any case, the crowd's perceptions will change; in their hearts the fear arising from the transgression they believe they witnessed will mingle with every nightmare they have ever had and with the archetypal horrors that are the culture's greatest fears, resulting in distortions and projections.

When they look at the women who have known Her kiss and who are Her kin, they will see the Scarlet Whore, and the corrupt will fear that she will spread corruption. When they look at the men who have known Her kiss, they will see the Beast, and the brutal and the greedy will fear that he will ravage and plunder. When they look at the ones who love Her who dance outside categories of masculinity and femininity, the ones who strive not to interact with anything that is not silicone or plastic, they will see Abomination and fear the unraveling of the natural order.

The crowd might turn on you gradually, or all at once. I am kin to the Oak, and the Oak draws lightning, so for me it was sudden. But slowly, or suddenly, turn they will and they will grab you and they will drag you with them in the direction that neither you nor they understood had always been their destination.

Soon you will realize that the road they have made for you leads into a court that accepts the evidence of the crowd's fears as proof of your guilt and from there to the place of your exile or your execution. When she sees you are on that road, She will whisper the same words to you that She whispered once to a Palestinian magician who was the consort of Her sister's priestess—"You will be hated because of my name but anyone who stands firm to the end will be saved."

Like him, you might repeat those words to the ones who have walked closest with you. By morning, most will deny you.

On the way up the hill where sacrifices are made, the crowd will strip you of your clothes, your possessions, your reputation, your name. While you die to who you were, some will spit on you, and some will mock you, and some will celebrate. If you are lucky, there will be a few with true hearts who have walked with you to the end of that awful road and will take your body down from the gallows tree and anoint you with oil and wrap you in a shroud and carry you to the entrance of the cave where you will lie in the time of darkness. But even they can go no further.

So it was for me.

At the entrance of the cave, I met my Wild Queen, clothed in white. She bent over and kissed me. Her kiss sealed the un-making of who I had been. As I entered the cave, she seemed colder, and sharper of tooth. I had forgotten that Bone Mother was her name in winter. Hers had become a terrifying beauty. Her kiss moved through me like frost moving over the land. Soon I was at the edge of sleep, and she whispered to me:

You let
the wrong people
dream you onto
the wrong road.
They dreamed
you broken
and bleeding
and dressed in rags,
they dreamed
you a stranger
with uncouth ways
and a barbarian's tongue,
they dreamed jagged rocks
and a wild storm,
and when they saw
your eyes
that had
gazed in
the abyss
they dreamed
you were a monster
born of its depths
and not the

wild King
who returned
from dark waters
bearing starlight.
But you gathered
the nine woods
and built yourself
a needfire,
by fire
you conjured
wind
that blew
away the clouds
to reveal the
Seven Hathor's
shining between
the horns
of the Celestial Bull
and the Hunter
who guides you
to the Milky Way
which you follow
though you ford
across rivers
of tears
and blood
onto a wild road.

I wake from a dream of the road the winds around the *fernie brae* to find myself in the cave. It is not clear how long I slept but my Wild Queen has not left my side. She is stirring a cauldron filled with my bones. I recognize what is happening. I am in a place of the dead, a place of unmaking that is also a place of initiation.

I know now that I have been there forty days. Forty days from Samhain to the Winter Solstice. The Tibetans say forty days from the time a soul leaves the body and finds its next incarnation

At Samhain, an axe fell, cutting me off from the life I had lived before. This has always been the way—the road onto which the people dream the King ends atop a high hill at Samhain. I was beneath the hill, among the dead though not of them, not yet ready to be reborn into the world.

The axe appears in the iconography of the stone carvings of the places where early kings were crowned in Ireland, suggesting one must survive a kind of death to become King, to become the bridegroom of the land. Dying, you are unmade, and must be made new. Archaeologist Gordon Noble says, "The axe undertaken may well have indicated the reciprocal relationship between kings and gods where shapeshifting and transfiguration were a necessary part of accessing the gods."

A cutting away of the old life, the old persona, the old identity is necessary to be made anew—and to enter the Otherworld, the dark, watery place of unmaking and remaking, the cavern that is both grave and womb.

Before the White Queen had carried me into the cave, her Ravens had stripped away my flesh. What was left was a skeleton of the person I had been. And now, even that will be broken down. My bones are being made into soup over a cooking fire in a cave between worlds.

When my bones have dissolved completely, my Wild Queen pours the broth down a shaft that reaches down to the Otherworld Well where all the waters of the world have their source.

I have been dispersed into its waters in a place where the only light that shines is the light of distant stars, ghost light of the furnaces in which the elements of my being had been forged illuminated the hidden pool where they now dance without form, rearranging themselves.

Here too, all the songs of the roots and the seeds and the dead that echo through the body of the Earth are amplified, calling the tune of the molecular dance of dissolving and reforming. The dance calls me through a thousand forms.

Moriarty said of this place: "It was at Connla's Otherworld well that I learned that being human is a habit that can be broken."

But if that habit can be broken, it can be relearned as well.

It was thus that Nuada regrew the arm cut off in battle that he might again fulfill the dream of his people. With no tuath, no tribe, no people left to dream me back into wholeness, I must instead become the dream of my ancestors and of the land itself. I must love the world enough to come fully home to my body. I must love my body and my being enough to know myself worthy to wed the Queen who is the embodied spirit of the forest and the hills and the wild waters.

When Orion is reflected in the pool, I come into my once and future form: the King who went to the Otherworld hunting wisdom, hunting knowledge, hunting all he needed to understand to be wedded to the land. As my eyes form, I close them for a moment and see those of my Beloved, the wild green of Beech leaves in May. I open them and begin swimming up a river back into the world, guided by the stars of Orion's belt, to come together with her in body again, and to walk together in the world.

My heart calls to her:

Though my body
drips still
with the dark waters
of rebirth,
they sparkle
like starlight
in the air
that still
shimmers
with the
strange
charge
of winter lightning.
I will
meet you
tonight
by a wild spring
that mirrors
Orion

and
the snow
tipped Firs.
In my cupped
hands
the waters
of remembering
and the
twinned
acorns
of an
ancient Oak

As I rise to the surface of that pool, I see her eyes. My Wild Queen, my Beloved come into human form. I emerge, still smelling of water and stone and darkness, and she wraps me in a Green Mantle. We have come home. Now to awaken our Kindred who sleep still beneath the Hollow Hills.

Waking the Daoine Sidhe

Poll na mBrón rises above the limestone and Heather and Gorse of the Burren in the west of Clare. The massive stones of the portal tomb mark the grave where an entire tribe buried its dead. They form a gate.

Standing before it, I can feel a wind blow through it from the other side of the veil, cold and dark as the space between stars. But I also see people gathered around the tomb in springtime, making love, their ecstasy feeding the land, and the gates of life opening so that the dead of the tribe might be born back through the bodies of the living and the life they give rise to. The new life is fed not just by the one who brings the sperm and the one whose egg inhabits the uterus of the body that will be the child's first world, but by the pleasure and exaltation of all engaged in the rite.

In the time of these rites, the stones were surrounded by ancient Oaks. That forest was cleared by invaders and its soil washed to the sea. Still, Hazel saplings try to grow back. Given the chance to grow into trees, their falling leaves would form the soil where acorns might sprout and take root.

Nothing is ever truly gone. Our homes, our settlements, our cities are built on the graveyards of worlds gone by—of forests, meadows, swamps, marshes, and deserts.

But anyone who has seen a feral weed growing up through a crack in the sidewalk knows that the seeds of those worlds gone by remain beneath the pavement and the concrete, waiting for water, air, and sun to call another generation into existence.

Herbalist Ryan Drum told me the story recently of a place in New England that had been deforested for over 200 years —cleared first for timber, then for farmland. But left alone, the fields began growing back into a forest. Before long, even before its food source appeared, Ghost Pipe re-emerged.

Ghost Pipe, an eerie white saprophytic plant, is notoriously hard to cultivate. The scientists watching the forest's return were baffled: where did the plant come from? Were there seeds in the soil just waiting to return? Or were the roots themselves dormant all that time, stirred back to life by the flow of nutrients between the trees taking root around them? One way or another, a plant that vanished from the above ground world we inhabit was waiting in the underworld to return.

In Chernobyl, when the people abandoned the town, the Birch Forest returned. So did the Wolves and the Deer. Is the same thing true of the parts of our humanity we pushed beneath the surface to survive the civilizing process? The forest of Chernobyl is now burning as it has become a battlefield. Can the rewilding of our sense of self remove the threat our resurgent violence brings to the rewilding of the land by bringing back ways that are "kinder and less civilized?"

In the story of my Irish ancestors, long before the invasion of the English (who pepper my ancestry too), came the arrival of the Gaels, the sons of my forefather Mil, and the war the waged against the Tuatha Dé, the tribe of the gods. They lived lives wedded to the land, and their songs could summon a storm or bring the sun's return.

The Tuath Dé had come to Ireland early in the history of the world, sailing on ships carried through the sky by the North Wind to wage a war to free the island from the brutal rule of Balor, a wicked king who demanded human sacrifice and whose single-eyed gaze corrupted and withered all it looked upon. In many ways, we can see him as the personification and embodiment of the spirit that would become first civilization, then empire, colonialism, and global capitalism, overrunning the world. The great sea god Mannanán was already there when the Tuath Dé arrived. He was one of the older, wilder gods who became their kin and their teacher. He trained his foster son, Lugh, in the martial and magical arts—Lugh blinded and slew Balor with a single thrust of a spear made of sunlight.

In the next wave of invasion, when the Gaels came to Ireland, knowing that their arrival would bring another round of destruction, the Tuath Dé summoned a great storm to drive back their ships. But the Gaelic bard Amergin, standing on the prow of a ship just beyond the ninth wave from the shore, sang a song to the land that spoke of his understanding of the unity of all things, of his memory of being a Stag with antlers of seven tines, a Salmon in a pool, a Hawk flying above the cliffs at the water's edge. With that song, he seduced the spirit of the land herself, and the wind and the rain and the waves ceased to obey the commands of the Tuath Dé. As the invaders' ships landed, the Hawthorn bloomed.

But not all who sailed on those ships had the same wisdom and reverence as their tribe's bard, and the ways they brought to Ireland were, to invert a phrase of Victor Anderson's, "more civilized and less kind." They brought the iron sword, the iron axe, the iron plough and the Tuath Dé could not abide the brutality of this new way of life.

By this time, Mannanán had become one of the kings of the Tuath Dé, even though he had not been born among them. He gathered his people under a mound at the mouth of the Boyne, the river that mirrors the Milky Way, and showed them another world below, the world from which all things in this world emerge, the world to which the dead return. He divided among them the Hollow Hills that were the common tombs of the Neolithic people of Ireland and showed them how to pass into the Otherworld from this world through the tombs. When they made that passage, the Tuath Dé became the Daoine Sidhe, the people of the mound.

He also taught them an incantation, Mannanán's Cloak, that allowed them to remain shrouded from human sight when they pass into this world. But like all things of wind and water and word, the cloak conjured is a fleeting thing, and like all cloaks, it sometimes slips.

Legend tells us that at the times of year when the gates between worlds are open, they move freely again in the middle world between the underworld and the heavens that we inhabit. Those who disrespect them can meet with horrendous fates. But, sometimes, when the Daoine Sidhe come across someone who greets them with reverence, who comes with an open heart, and in whom they recognize something kindred, they show tremendous generosity, sharing secrets of magic and medicine long ago lost to cultures who forgot their connection to the underworld and their place in the dance of life and death.

Is this history literal or metaphorical? That distinction only makes sense if you believe that only one thing can be true at a time. As I write in *The Forest Reminds Us Who We Are*:

> What we call the literal is an attempt to impose a single set of colonial metaphors on the world.
>
> Manannán mac Lir, son of the Irish sea god, sees the ocean as a field of wildflowers. Dogen saw mountains as slowly moving rivers of stone and rivers as swiftly moving mountains of water. I see all these things and more.
>
> When you experience the world as alive, it is not mere whimsy to equate a river and a galaxy, both are alive and flowing.

The dead travel across the Milky Way. It is mirrored by the Boyne.

So, these stories are the stories of what happened to our ancestors, those Neolithic builders of dolmens and megaliths who now sleep beneath the hollow hills. And they are also the story of what has happened to us.

We emerge from the dark, watery womb of our mothers where there is no separation into a world of a hundred thousand forms. We become fragments in a fragmented world, alienated from the rest of life. We are trained to see ourselves as discrete individuals. That individuality is not false but it is also not the only truth.

Eco-psychologist Challis Glendinning speaks of the way in which traditional cultures live embedded within what she calls the Primal Matrix:

> "The state of a healthy, wholly functioning psyche in full bodied participation with the healthy earth. Our Primal Matrix grew from the earth, is inherently part of the earth, and is built to thrive in intimacy with the earth."

The Oaxacan scholar Gustavo Echeva says that the difference between a colonized worldview and an Indigenous worldview is that from an Indigenous perspective, "the first layer of being is we."

That state remains available to us if we are willing to let go of the guilt, shame, and fear that serve to separate us from it. But to access it, we have to face those specters. And it is in part the seeming reality of these thought forms infused with intense emotion that gives us our fear of the dark and of the underworld.

The greatest of these fears is the fear of losing our consciousness and individuality which comes from believing so strongly that we are the personalities we have inhabited since childhood. Accessing anything beneath the level of our personality threatens to flood us with experiences that could shatter us. But that is a story told by a culture that depends on our being cut off from the fullness of who we are. In order to avoid being robbed of our individual lives through jail, and ostracization, or the gun, we learn to conform to the will of some disembodied inorganic whole with no roots in the soil or the soul—a gang, a church, a corporation, a nation. We are tricked into sacrificing both what is most unique about us and what connects us to all of life.

The reality is that we can experience both our individuality and our deep connection with All Things simultaneously. The fungal realm gives us a clear illustration of how this can work. When we think of mushrooms, we think of the fleshy tissues that grow above the ground, the mushroom's fruiting body which serves to gather nourishment and information from the world around it. If we see two fruiting bodies of the same species six inches apart, we think of them as two separate beings, which they are in a way.

But there is another reality too. The fruiting bodies of the mushrooms are only the above ground part of the organism. Underground, they are connected by vast mycelial networks that carry information and exhibit a complex consciousness of their own. Those mycelial fibers intertwine with the roots of trees and wildflowers, and together they form the mind of the forest.

In the same way, our own physical bodies are vessels of an individual consciousness and are necessary for us to do work here in the middle realm between the heavens and the underworld, the world in which physical change, physical sensation, and physical pleasure are possible.

When that individual consciousness is tapped into the Primal Matrix, that experience, that sensation, that pleasure becomes fed and watered by the deep ecstasy of a universe falling in love with Herself as she experiences Herself through our bodies. The part of us that knows how to tap into that matrix is the part we have exiled to the underworld, the part that feels unsafe in our own bodies when our ways of living and knowing are not guided by compassionate wisdom of the heart. The iron blade and the iron plough drove our ancestors beneath the hollow hills, carrying with them things that are fundamental to the wholeness of the world. But like that ancient Bear King, Arthur, whose body was borne across the water from Wales to Brittany, they are not dead and gone; they are only sleeping, waiting to return in the hour when the world needs them most.

We carry blessings and curses from our ancestors hidden in our DNA. The experiences of one generation live on in the bodies of the next. Myriad experiences of hundreds of generations come together to shape what we feel, what we know, and who we are.

My own Autistic genetics carry traits that science now traces back to the earliest generations of humans, back in the time when some Homo sapiens fell in love with Neanderthals and Denisovans and created something of uncanny wonder in the alchemical alembics of their wombs. Journalist Steve Silberman writes:

> "In recent years, researchers have determined that most cases of autism are not rooted in rare de novo mutations but in very old genes that are shared widely in the general population while being concentrated more in some families than in others. Whatever autism is it is not a product of modern civilization. It is a strange gift from our deep past, passed down through millions of years of evolution."

What is the nature of this strange gift? The one thing all autistic people appear to have in common is an unusual brain structure, where synapses proliferate rapidly in non-linear ways, resulting in minds that make novel sets of associations between seemingly unrelated things. We read the patterns in the world be they in the arrangement of train schedules, the movement of clouds, the lines of computer code, or the course of human history.

We also experience emotion and sensation intensely, and the gates of our senses are open to a much wider array of information than those of other humans. This means we can find sublime pleasure or excruciating pain from textures and tastes and sights and sounds and scents that others may not notice at all. It also means we can simultaneously sense the emotions others have hidden deep inside, and thus fail to follow the social rules that dictate the expected responses to words, actions, and facial expressions. Our empathy also extends beyond the human realm to include plants, animals, and machines.

People can achieve similar neurological states by immersing themselves in the wilderness or by ingesting certain plants, chemicals, or fungi, but those states are somewhat transitory, whereas Autism is permanent. Give an Autistic person an eighth of an ounce of Liberty Cap mushrooms and send them out into the forest, they will most likely come back mad, dead, or a poet.

The chances of coming back a poet were much higher in the times when such initiations followed training by someone who saw patterns in the world and felt more at home in the company of Oaks and Ravens than in the hubbub of the village market. This was possible when the community recognized that it needed someone who could mediate between them and the gods, the plants, the animals, the land, the stars, the wind, the rain, the ancestors, the descendants, and the Other Crowd. The strange folk at the edge of the village were often considered kin to the ones who slept beneath the Hollow Hills and were said to carry traces of faerie blood.

With the coming of capitalism and the industrial age, most people stopped seeing the value of experiencing and perceiving the world in unusual ways. Stories gathered in the Irish countryside in the 19th century give instructions for detecting a changeling child, a faerie among humans who must be killed for the good of the family: uncanny expressions, a strange gaze that seems to be looking into another world, and precocious knowledge and speech. The traits are an almost exact match for the diagnostic criteria for Asperger's Syndrome in the DSM-IV. Nevertheless, some have survived to keep passing down those genes, and in the 60s and 70s, something quite unexpected happened: thousands of people underwent unguided psychedelic initiations. Some went mad. Some died. But what happened with some of the others changed the world.

Many of those who "passed the acid test" were people whose thinking was already divergent from the cultural norm. Among them were strange, brilliant people who found their way into science, mathematics, and engineering. In the realm of mathematics, this era produced chaos theory. Chaos theory examines the nature of complex, dynamic systems whose operation follows an innate logic but not a linear one, and the role of very small changes having very big results—the proverbial beating of the butterfly's wings in Brazil that creates a hurricane in Texas. Together with quantum entanglement, which speaks of the ways twinned particles mirror and influence each other across vast distances, it provides the basis for an understanding of the operation of magic in the universe. (Consistent both with Victor Anderson's insight that magic itself is a science, and Arthur C. Clarke's insight that any sufficiently advanced technology will appear to be magic to those unaccustomed to its operation.)

Speaking of the 17th century, the era that gave form and focus to a rationalism bent on driving wildness and otherness and magic from the world, James Hillman wrote "Once the earth was declared dead, the autopsy could begin in earnest." Chaos theory tore the fabric of 17th century rationalist materialism to shreds, revealing nature to be fluid and complex, though not without pattern. This lay the groundwork for James Lovelock's Gaia hypothesis, the idea that the earth itself is a single self-regulating system—in other words, a life form. A *New York Times* op-ed recently described the rise of a postmodern animism in the realms of biology and climate science.

During this same era, the ultimate embodiment and expression of the goals of the culture that arose from the rationalist materialism of the 17th century, the U.S. military inadvertently crafted a Pandora's box that operates on these same principles. They hired creative thinkers, many of them Autistic, to solve the problem of developing a communications system that could continue to operate even if a nuclear attack destroyed some of its major hubs.

Terrence McKenna would later write that the CIA had made two great mistakes: LSD and the internet. The two are not unrelated. Many of the people involved in the development and evolution of the internet relied on LSD or psychedelic mushrooms to further potentiate their creativity. Both are related to the fungal realm: LSD is derived from a compound produced by Ergot, a fungus that grows on Rye and likely was used in initiation ceremonies by Greek Mystery schools. Not surprisingly, these scientists and engineers, working symbiotically with fungi, created a replica of a mycelial network.

At first glance, it appears to be the perfect system for engaging in universal surveillance in the service of what the military calls 'full spectrum dominance.' But complex systems have a mind of their own. That synthetic simulacrum of the mycelium connects human minds with each other, strengthening the influence of the collective consciousness (and the collective unconscious) on the individual. The nature of that collective mind has less to do with the intentions of its creators than with the synthesis of the thoughts and emotions the system is fed.

As the language of the "computer virus" suggests, the internet can be a vector for the transmission of contagion. But remember, not all viruses are harmful. We are now beginning to understand that viruses actually play a role in facilitating evolution by changing our DNA. A virus is a tiny thing that can effect massive changes in a much larger system. The internet has spread hate and disinformation. Yet it also has exposed billions to the image of the Earth as seen from space, the voices and experiences of people from around the world, and the sense that we are, indeed, one people and one planet, one organism—albeit one sometimes caught in fever dreams.

Those who speak of and with the faerie realm often suggest the sense of a hive mind held together by the consciousness of its Wild Queen. Her kiss can be the vector of transmission through which the ancient consciousness re-enters the world. It is like the forked hummingbird tongue that, seeking nectar, opens the flower of the heart.

The heart is not a pump, it is a drum. Like all things that vibrate rhythmically, it generates a strong electromagnetic field that can pull other electromagnetic fields into resonance. Its natural tendency is to move into resonance with the field generated by the flow of iron in the Earth's core. (The science of this is described in Stephen Buhner's *The Secret Teachings of Plants*).

There are entrances to the hollow hills that lie within us. The Queen's kiss sets the heart beating in a rhythm that opens the gates of those entrances and wakes the sleeping ones who lie beyond them.

She awaits you, as she awaited me, beneath the blooming Hawthorn. The price of the kiss is your life. The gift of her kiss is your life, and the life of the world.

A Walk in the Woods

In late summer, I went walking among the woods with my friend and teacher, Cornelia Benavidez, Victor Anderson's biographer. Cornelia had met and befriended Victor in the dark days following Gwydion Pendderwen's death and over the two decades that followed, he shared with her his understanding of the world. Now, as we walked among the Pines, she passed some of those insights on to me.

Victor told her that people must understand that if we do not wake up to the damage that we do to ourselves and each other, we will fall even further from the grace that has been bought for us.

"This grace was bought by the sacrifice of the Christos and others. If we refuse to open our eyes, we shall slide even deeper into the hell of our own making," she said.

"What a fearful pronouncement! What does it mean?" I asked

Cornelia explained, "Victor saw most of humanity as sexually and emotionally crippled, and because of this is so warped and hamstrung we cannot see the love and beauty that surrounds us. Instead we treat all forms of it with suspicion or disdain. Beauty thus becomes a distraction, a temptation, and an illusion of good, while love and sex are rejected and mocked as the mundane mockery of the real love of God. Mutilation and death then becomes the solution to everything. A child loses its hand for stealing, a teen girl gets stoned for being raped or she is executed or imprisoned for life for trying to defend herself. We send boys and young men off to war both justly and unjustly. We allow conditions to exist where the innocent die, all these are sacrifices and the more blood was spilled, the more twisted we became."

"What did Victor know of how all this sacrifice begin?" I asked.

"He said that the early idea of sacrifice was not to give blood to the God but someone to the world of the dead to commune with ancestors, spirits, or the Goddess because of great need. Kings and chieftains, shamans and elders offered themselves up as messengers for the people. Criminals gave their lives as payment for their crimes so they could be reborn and serve the tribe better in the next life.

They walked out into the snow or drank poison or jumped off a cliff. Life was precious and short. People needed each other and most believed that they were coming back.

But then people got greedy, and the nasty idea was born that maybe spilling blood was a way to get things done. The more innocent blood was shed, the more they demanded."

"So, where does Victor think this is leading us?" I asked, though I feared the answer.

"Victor says the unthinkable and bizarre becomes more acceptable just as it became such in Nazi Germany. Now, the growing symptoms of this reemerging illness are all around us. It shows itself in our children cutting themselves and wanting to or even committing suicide. In our pagan traditions, many are being led by the nose to the same mistakes of past times and repeating them instead of moving forward. This leads to more debauchery and wickedness that repowers the cult of sacrifice instead of leaving it behind.

"We already feel the emptiness of all joy being drained from the Earth till all is nothing. Then evil will have won its day and it will take billions of years and more suffering to right it. This will be a great tragedy and sorrow for all Divine beings and us as we will stand in shame before them."

'Then where is hope?' I inquired.

Cornelia laughed, "It is in you! And in every child, in lovers in love, in every doting Grandparent, in the lion that washes her cub, in every tree and flower reaching to the sun! Hope grows like a weed in the heart and spirit of man, it but needs a little nourishment and those willing to carry it."

Cornelia then reminded me of some other matters that Victor spoke of:

"He said that the Hawaiian word *Aloha* is not only a greeting or goodbye but embodies the love that all people can feel for each other. Victor pointed out that this kind of love naturally and easily obeys the responsibilities and obligations we should have toward each other. This is not entrapment nor is it some sort of slavery but simply the pleasure of doing right my each other. Sure, in Hawaiian history they battled and quarreled as our Gods of Old did. The Hawaiians battled for Kingship and for territory, but it was unthinkable, unmanly without honor to commit rape. Therefore, such criminal conduct rarely happened."

"Yet, the Hawaiians practiced human sacrifice." I said.

Cornelia then spoke of how Victor explained to her and her friend in Hawaii that this is a deeper and more complex subject then people think.

"The Polynesians who first came to Hawaii came for several reasons, but one was to leave the practice of human sacrifice behind, and they did until it was reintroduced by a priest from the South Seas. Still, there was a difference between the Kahuna that makes her bed in front of a lava flow praying to save her village and being willing to lay down her life or be saved as the Gods will, then those that mindlessly kill prisoner after endless prisoner, calling such slaughter sacred. This is not any different than the modern way of lining up the village and machine-gunning its people down.

"Can you see now why it became fairly easy for the Hawaiian mind to accept Jesus? The God who sacrificed himself -- what a wonder! Jesus, the Divine son, died like a human so that no one else would need to sacrifice again, not even animals. You see now why those of Hawaiian understanding look with horror upon the world that does not understand this. We cry and suffer by ignorance and by the arrogance that spits in the face of the Goddess's grace and mercy to re-invoke the wrath and rage of the God upon us all. Indigenous and aware people, our people, all over the planet know this and understand this. For us to really be free is to embrace truth and see things as they really are. Then people will finally understand what Jesus meant when he said the truth will set you free."

In her words I heard the echoes of my Indigenous Irish ancestors. In their history lay clues that would deepen my own understanding.

The Forest and the Trees

"Sé do bheatha, a bhean ba léanmhar
do bé ár gcreach tú bheith i ngéibhinn
do dhúiche bhreá i seilbh meirleach"[4]
—Padraig Pearse

When first I came to Ireland, the forests of the place I then called home along the Columbia River were burning while I was a continent and an ocean away. My heart recited a litany: *Cedar and Douglas Fir. Mountain Lion and Deer. Black Bear and Salmon. Devil's Club and Wild Ginger.*

In another time, fire was part of the land's cycle of life and death and rebirth. But the 1940's brought the cutting of the old growth forests to make ships for the U.S. Navy. Then came the housing booms of the 50's and 90's. Then climate change. The forest was no longer resilient as it once was, and nobody knows what is to come. And I, its priest, was so far away,

4. These words, from the marching song of the 1916 uprising in Ireland, roughly translate to "Hail, woman who has suffered so! It is our shame that you were in bondage, and your beautiful land was taken by thieves while we sold you to the invaders."

walking in the footsteps of my ancestors, trying to remember how to sing the wild back into the world.

When I first came to the rainforests of the Pacific, my ancestors told me "This is what our land was like before they took our forests."

Ireland, too, was once a place where great trees grew from soil fed by the bodies of Salmon dragged from the waters by Eagles. Though early agriculture did take its toll on the wilderness, the Brehon laws protected sacred trees and insisted on both reparations and physical restoration for even the stripping of too much bark from one.

The erosion of that protection began with the Norman invasion in the 12th century, an incursion sanctioned by the Pope in the name of wiping out "barbarism" in a country where women headed many of the households and churches, where the clergy wasn't celibate, and where wild places had legal standing. In a move that would be echoed by British colonizers in North America, Norman invaders exploited the cultural differences in understandings of land ownership. Irish historian Eoin Neeson writes:

> "In England, the Normans had introduced the notion of 'forests' (a term that simply meant a large area of land, not necessarily all wooded) as areas where a special law applied. The Irish idea of land title was very different from the Norman one of absolute ownership, and this much facilitated the Normans. When an Irish lord or King donated land to one of his subjects, he gave not ownership, but dominion subject to recall. Therefore, the Irish nobleman who 'gave' land to a Norman was allowing a rescindable dominion in trust. When he learned that the Norman thought otherwise

> and was prepared to fight for it, the Irish lord fought back, or agreed to the Norman authority under what he saw as duress."

For a few more centuries, the British would lack the power and will to impose their models of religion and land ownership in Ireland in earnest. That all changed in the 17th century, as British coffers swelled with gold looted by the Spanish from the Americas and it grew hungry for expansion.

As the British Empire formed, Ireland represented a source of untapped resources, a place where land and title could be given to an emerging moneyed class, and a dangerous example of another way of life to the British aristocracy and the nascent bourgeoisie. Elizabeth the First ordered the wholesale destruction of Ireland's forests to deny cover to Irish rebels—a foreshadowing of the U.S. use of Agent Orange in Vietnam—and to provide timber for naval ships and slave ships and charcoal for the furnaces of the nascent industrial age. Later that century, Cromwell escalated the brutality of the occupation, bringing near-genocidal levels of violence, pioneering many of the counter-insurgency techniques that the U.S. would use when it inherited Britain's imperial mantle.

I spent three days in the woods at the edge of the Burren, one of the last remnants of the wild Irish forest. Fern and Moss, Deer and Owl, ancient well and wild spring, Hawthorn and Blackthorn. The wheel has turned from Lughnasadh toward Samhain.

The whisper of the wind in the trees, the scent of rich dark soil and rotting leaves, the call of the Owl at dusk stir memories I never knew my body held of the Salmon run, the Deer hunt, the gathering of the Hazelnuts. But these are only memories for the land here, too.

The Oak and Birch Forest gives way to a wild Heather meadow, but at its edge is a tree plantation, Sitka Spruce grown for timber and kept alive with pesticides and fertilizers that filter into the waters that once teamed with Salmon and Trout.

What dies when a forest dies? Trees are memory keepers. Their bodies hold the trace of everything that has happened on the land throughout their lives. Even the degraded form of science emerging from a capitalist culture that denies the life of the world knows how to read the rings on the stump of a felled tree—or a core sample drilled from a living one—to divine the history of drought and flood and fire. Older sciences and emergent ones understand how to learn deeper, richer stories from living trees. But rows of trees are not forests. A forest is a living system of plants and animals and fungi woven together by mycorrhizal, pheromonal, and phytochemical exchanges; wild currents of sex and death.

When the Oak forests of western Ireland fell to the axes of the Queen of England's men, the soil too was lost, and the Burren became a landscape of thin soil covering the limestone of an ancient seabed. Seeds of Arctic plants left by the glaciers of the last Ice Age began to sprout. Yet, even in this transformed landscape, the wild world left to its own devices will sprout Willow and Birch whose leaves and branches would feed the soil, preparing for the Oaks' return. Civilization just needs to get out of the way.

Beyond the Pale

My people come from beyond the Pale. An Pháil Shasanach, the English Pale, was the area around Dublin that came under English occupation following the first British invasion in 1169.

Dublin had been established as a Viking outpost a century earlier. The Vikings encouraged marriage and cultural sharing with the Irish and with the traders and travelers from distant lands who came to the nascent city. The British did not.

The Irish language, Irish clothing, and even Irish hairstyles were forbidden within the Pale. As resistance built beyond the Pale, the British built a border wall, a series of fences and ditches to separate their area of control and influence from the rest of the island.

In 1580, warriors under the leadership of the great chieftain Fiach Mac Aodh Ó Broin succeeded in driving British troops who had advanced westward back across the Pale. A century later, armed with the latest artillery, Oliver Cromwell and his troops reclaimed control of much of the country for the British crown through a scorched earth campaign that approached the level of genocide.

Some would argue that the area that was once the Pale still bears the mark of occupation, though the last British troops left in 1922. The great Irish labor leader, James Connolly (Séamas Ó Conghaile), warned before his execution in 1916 that:

> "If you remove the English army tomorrow and hoist the green flag over Dublin Castle, unless you set about the organization of the Socialist Republic your efforts would be in vain. England would still rule you. She would rule you through her capitalists, through her landlords, through her financiers, through the whole array of commercial and individualist institutions she has planted in this country and watered with the tears of our mothers and the blood of our martyrs."

A century later, Ireland has become a tax haven for multinational corporations while the streets of Dublin are lined with the branches of big banks while more and more people become homeless.

Historically, the British saw the Irish who lived beyond the Pale as dangerous barbarians. To this day, the phrase in English means "unacceptable." My ancestors were the people this phrase first described.

My Mother's great grandmother was a Faolin, descended from a tribe of shapeshifting warriors who wore wolf skins and worshipped the ancient god, Crom Cruach, long after the coming of Christianity. None of her stories of Ireland have survived, but she did pass down the Sight.

Most of what I do know of my Irish ancestors comes from my Da's people, the O'Donoghues. The O'Donoghue Kings once ruled the area around Killarney (Cuille Airne—"Church of the Blackthorn Berry") in County Kerry, which remained a hotbed of resistance to British rule well into the 20th century. They were a sept of the Eóghanacht tribe, the tribe of the Kings of Munster, who had come from Cork to the shores of Lough Léin and their forests of Oak and Yew in the chaos that followed the death of King Brían Ború. They built a castle there from which to defend their new home.

Donn is the Gaelige word for "brown," and the name O'Donoghue (originally spelled Ó Donnchú) is derived from the Old Irish Ó Donnchada, which is usually translated as "Grandson of the Brown Warrior." But Donn is also the name of a god who was once mortal, a man who drowned and then became lord of the house of the dead—some say he is the dark twin of Lugh. Another interpretation of the Ó Donnnchada is "Warrior, Grandson of Donn." I came to this understanding intuitively as a child reading about Donn in a dusty old volume of the Encyclopedia Britannia. Rod O'Donoghue, the founder of the O'Donoghue Society which seeks to preserve our family history, came to a similar conclusion after much research. In his book, Heroic Landscapes, he wrote that "There was a family cult surrounding Donn, the god of the dead" and that the devotions of that family cult may have given rise to the "creation in spirit form" of one of the tribe's kings.

The king, Donal O'Donoghue, was in many ways the paragon of an Eóghanact King, with the kings of that tribe being fierce warriors who were none the less known for their wise and gentle ways. Rod O'Donoghue writes:

> "Donal is described as a man of great stature and good looks. He was just, generous, and wise, and a fearsome warrior sworn to fight any oppressor. He rode his white silver-shod horse with daring until one day later in his life he was unseated—to the amazement of his companions. He retreated to his library and dedicated himself to becoming a black magician, with the ability to transform into other shapes. After seven weeks, he explained to his curious wife what he was doing, he asked her for help. However [, ...] she needed to be tested, if she made a sound he would be taken from her forever. She agreed and he began to read from his black book. Frightful things were manifested, and his wife maintained her silence until the image of her own child lying dead on the table appeared and she screamed. [. .] The castle shook to its foundations. The O'Donoghue leapt from the window and disappeared into Lough Léin."

He had learned, to paraphrase Moriarty, that being human is a habit that can be broken. Shapeshifting is one of the oldest ways to come to know the unity and sacredness of all things. To be able to return to human form requires being anchored to this world and one's own form by "perfect love and perfect trust." This is, perhaps, another aspect of the mystery of sacral kingship, the need for the Shaman-King to be wedded to She Who Embodies the Land. In the tale of Tam Lin, Janet's perfect love allowed Tam Lin to return to this world from the Otherworld. But in the case of Donal O'Donoghue, the smallest crack in that perfect trust cut the thread that linked him to the world of the living.

The cloak that separates the world slips from time to time, especially at Sahmain and Bealtaine. Some say that Donal O'Donoghue still rises from Lough Léin on a white horse with a retinue of Otherworldly courtiers at dawn on the first of May every seven years.

The castle he built remained a bastion of resistance to the occupation of Ireland until it was taken by British troops in 1652, but the legacy of Donal O'Donoghue remained alive. A King, as Moriarty said, is the dream of a people. And the dream of a people does not always die with the body of the King. The Irish have always called on the honored dead—be they Kings or Queens or Heroes or Saints—to help them in times of need. One could argue that in its oldest sense, the Irish word "Dé" which means both "god" and "puff of smoke" likely originally referred to the ancestors who answered the people's prayers and the smoke of the offerings burned to invoke them. In that sense, Donal O'Donoghue became a god. There are tales of his coming, centuries after his death, to the aid of poor farmers harassed by cruel landlords, keeping his vow to defend the oppressed. One 19th century folklorist spoke of "Daniel O'Donoghue, the Faerie King of Munster," with Daniel being an anglicization of Donal and the name of my great-grandfather, on whose hundredth birthday I was born. His parents would have known the tales of the great King and in many ways, their naming of him predicted part of the course his life would take.

Growing up in the shadow of our ancestral castle, my great grandfather came of age in the late 19th century, born in the wake of the Great Hunger where the British allowed a million

Irish to starve when the potato crops they were growing to supply their colonizers' hunger failed, and half a generation before the Easter rebellion of 1916. He was part of a movement and generation influenced by the ancient tales of the Fianna,[5] bands of warriors living in the forest who were sworn to defend the poor and the weak. The poor were all around, and the threat to them came from police and soldiers who came to the door to drive people out of their homes when they were late on the rent to the absentee landlords who held title to their ancestral homesteads and who beat people in public for speaking Gaelige. He became Captain in the Irish Republican Brotherhood (*Bráithreachas Phoblacht na hÉireann*), a secret organization dedicated to the revival of the Irish language and culture and the liberation of the country from occupation. The British crown put a price on his head, and for that he fled the country at the age of 21.

He ended up in Lynn, MA, where for the rest of his life he stayed atop the highest hill in the city so then he could always look down and see who was coming. There he met a woman who had grown up a few miles up the road from him, Nora O'Meara. No one who knew her remembered ever hearing her speak a word of English, even when her eldest son, my Great Uncle, Jiggs, and his wife Tessie were the only living Gaelige speakers left in her world.

When danger did come, it came from the Ku Klux Klan. My grandfather remembered the Klan burning a cross a few

5. Their name is related to the Gaelige words for "wild" and "Deer" and to the name of the great warrior King, Fionn mac Cumhaill, who founded the first of these bands.

blocks from his apartment on High Rock Tower, terrorizing a neighborhood of immigrants who had fled war and occupation.

Though his mother never spoke a word of English to him, my grandfather remembered no Gaelige from his childhood. The loss of a language is common in families and communities in a strange and hostile land.

When I visit my great grandparents in the cemetery in Lynn, I speak to them in broken Gaelige. Something of their inheritance awakens in me, my body remembers stories nobody living has the words to tell.

Fifteen years ago, my Da went to Tullig, the area of Killarney the Captain was from to see what he could find out about his great grandfather's life. He had the names of some second and third cousins there. And, really, most of the people whose families have been there for more than a generation or two are related to us somehow. But no one would answer his questions.

On the last night, a woman told him "People here don't like to talk."

"Yes, but you and I both know you're my cousin," he replied.

"Go to Countess Bridge," she said, "then you will understand."

Today my Da sent me a picture of the plaque on the Countess Bridge. In the wake of the uprising that began in 1917, the Irish Free State agreed to allow the British to continue to occupy the areas of Ulster that had a Protestant majority, the result of colonized and displaced Scots being installed as overseers in Ireland a couple of centuries earlier, in exchange for home rule. Civil war broke out in 1922. The Irish Republican Army separated from the Irish Free State and took up arms to fight for a united, decolonized Ireland. Kerry was a hotbed of their resistance.

In March 1923, the Irish Free State launched a series of brutal reprisals against the IRA in retaliation for a bombing. On March 7, two relatives of mine—Jeremiah O'Donoghue and another Daniel O'Donoghue—and two other IRA soldiers, Stephen Buckley and Timothy Murphy, were tied to the bridge and the bridge was blown up, killing them.

The IRA surrendered that May and would remain largely dormant until 1969 when a nonviolent Civil Rights movement in Northern Ireland faced violent repression from the British military and the Protestant majority, and a new generation took up arms again.

I don't know what the captain himself lived through. I know beatings, torture, arbitrary executions, and a cruel "residential school" system like the one imposed on Indigenous communities in Canada and the U.S. were features of the British occupation of Ireland in the late 19th century. And I know there are reasons why people don't talk about what happened.

We carry our ancestors' experiences with us. In our family cultures and in our DNA. In a passage I was reading just before Da sent me the picture of the memorial, Sharon Stanley writes:

> "The hidden social and neurological dynamics of trauma do not die with the person who directly encountered the event. Rather, the remnants of trauma live on through ordinary, yet

> highly significant survival patterns, including silence about the trauma."

What we do with that trauma has impacts across time and space.

Breaking the silence, questioning the patterns, and feeling into the history gives us an opportunity to profoundly change the ways in which we engage the world. When the trauma we inherit goes unnamed and unexamined, it plays itself either in the form of numbness and disconnection or in the form of fear and aggression that doesn't know the source or origin.

When we engage and work with that trauma, it has the opportunity to move and heal and move again towards resolution —making us freer to be more fully embodied, present, and connected to the living world around us, and to reclaim what came before the trauma. Solid ground on which to make our stand.

My ancestors lived beyond the Pale. And so do I.

Of Fire and Rain

Ancient Oaks and Yews survived in Killarney long after Cromwell's time but the eradication of Wolves meant that the Red Deer had no natural predators left, and the Red Deer overgrazed Oak saplings and undergrowth. In late April 2021, wildfires ripped through the forests around Lough Léin, just days before An O'Donoghue Mór was scheduled to rise from his palace beneath the waters.

Distraught, I called out to him and to the gods and ancestors of his people and mine, my prayers mingling with those of thousands around the world who love that forest:

Sleeper beneath the waters,
Magician King,
the stars and the Whitethorn
mark the coming
of your emergence,
but now the flames call you,

the forest calls you.
your descendants call you
to wake before
the May Tree blooms:

A O'Dhonnchaid Mór,
I am your descendant,
born 100 years
after the last
of my line
to call these burning forests home.

Is mise Seán
mac Brían
mac Donnchadh
mac Domhnal
mac Seán
mac Pádraig
ui Donnchadh

In the name
of my father's
father's father.
in the name
of the forest,
in the name
of the land,

I summon
you now
wake from
your slumber

and call the
waters above you
to become
the rain
that will
cool the flames.

A Eóghain Mór
A Mhuig Nuadat,
high born one,
Salmon's kin
God-servant and King,

is mise Eóghanact,
I am your descendant,
born on a distant shore
in your name.
and the name
of the spirits
who dwell
within the rath
that was our people's home,

I beseech you
to call forth the rains
to quell the fires
that burn the forest
of my ancestors' home.

A Bhrigid of the shining flame
Bhrigid of the ancient wells,
is mise do dhraoi, do fhile, do mhic,

call back the fires
and call down the waters
that the forest might live
and grow
and be reborn

A Medb of the honeyed lips,
is mishe do dhraoi, do fhile, do leannán,

kiss the scorched earth
that it might bloom again

A Mhannanáin of the silver bough
A Mhannanáin of the ocean's depths
A Mhannanáin of the winter stars
is mishe do dhraoi, do fhile, do shliocht,

teach me the songs
that will wake the ancestors,
that will stir the roots,
that will wake the Oak
within the acorn,

that your world
and this world
might live again.

In the days that followed, help came first in the form of helicopters, one coming from Scotland, pouring water on the flames, and then through merciful rains. Many ancient trees were lost but much of the forest remains and, if we allow it to, will grow again.

We Forgot That We Were Kings

My ancestors whisper: "When they took our Goddesses and turned them into plaster and put them behind the communion rail, we forgot that we were Kings."

The men of my line once claimed Sovereignty by wedding She who embodied the living spirit of the mountains and rivers and hills. But when the old ways of Kingship are lost and the land calls you to be her Wild Lover, how can you respond?

That question has haunted the men of Ireland and of the Irish diaspora for centuries. Again, and again, the wrong answer has cost them their lives.

In ancient Ireland, on the hill of Tara, it was the stones themselves who communicate the Will of the land, proclaiming who was fit to be King. Before the stones would allow the one who would be King to pass, he must become the lover of She Who Dwells Beneath the Hollow Hills, she who embodies and weaves together the consciousness of the land itself, the dreams whispered among mycelia and roots, the songs that arise from the cold waters below, she by whose desires kings and chieftains rise and fall.

Describing the ascent of the great King, Cormac mac Art, Moriarty writes:

> "First, in a manner most sacred, he must marry Meadhbh, the goddess of sovereignty. Meadbh was dangerous and strange. Could be, you would look at her and she would be the ugliest and foulest thing you could imagine. Turning away in utter, sickening revulsion, you would for some reason be tempted to look back and now she would be fair beyond anything you could imagine. The one who was destined to be King must be able to live with her foul and fair."

Tradition is unclear on whether Meadbh is one of the Daoine Sidhe, or if she came before them, but her shapeshifting ways reflect the fluid nature of embodiment in the faerie realms, and the call to kiss the hag who becomes a beautiful woman, or the beautiful woman who becomes the hag, is an old test of the purity of the heart of one who would wed the land itself, becoming sovereign.

The great feminist philosopher and psychoanalyst, Julia Kristeva, speaks of the ways in which the horror of the abject and the beauty of the sublime break open our frames of reference, forcing us into engagement with that which language cannot contain, disrupting the Law of the Father, the old order of understanding. For a new King to emerge from the land is for the old order to be broken. When the emergent law ossifies, it will be time for it to be broken again by another who is willing to transgress it by embracing what it renders abject and experiencing it as sublime.

When Meadbh has taken the new King as lover, the stones themselves provide the outward earthly signs of the completion of the sacrament. Moriarty writes:

> "There were at Tara two thunderous standing stones called Blocc and Bluigne, with only a hand's breadth between them. They too must accept the one who would be King, opening before the chariot horses, letting him ride regally through."

Having passed between them, one more test remains. Moriarty writes:

> "There is in Tara, a standing, stone phallus called Fal. The one who would be King must ride pass it and if, as he does so, it doesn't screech against his chariot, he is rejected."

Why must the King be sexually initiated by 'She Who Sleeps Beneath the Hollow Hills' and then welcomed to the site of his coronation by the stones that are the bones of the land?

The Irish word *rí* held a different set of connotations than are suggested by our modern usage of the English word "King." The etymology of both words suggests something of the nature of older understanding of kingship. The Irish word *rí* comes from the Proto-Indo-European word "*href*," which when used as a verb meant "to right oneself" and when used as an adjective, "just." The *rí* is the one who is able to right himself in relation to the world around him and thus act justly. The word

"King" derives from the word "kin." The King is the one who holds kin together and who is kindred to all. Jason Kirkey tells us that in an early Irish context:

> "The King was someone who knew his place in the world. His power was derived from the land and the people. It was the King's Fírrinne, his ability to uphold the proper order of all things, which allowed him to ensure the health and fertility of the land and peace among the people. He was less a ruler and more a maintainer of the natural order."

"Fírrinne" literally translates as "truth."

The King is the lover and consort of She Who Rules from Below. He is also her voice and her embodiment in the world above. In ancient Ireland, it was customary to suck the King's nipples—an act we might well read as symbolic of receiving nourishment from the body of the King. When he is healthy, the land and the people and his Otherworld Queen are fed by his vitality. When he speaks Her will into law, all is harmonious and just. His is a tongue that cannot lie.

His life belongs to the land and to the people. If he is faithful, when he dies, he will be buried beneath the Hollow Hills, returning to the arms of his wild lover. Perhaps he will be born again among his people. But what happens when the Old Ways have been outlawed and all but forgotten? How, then, does a man receive the call of She Who Rules from Below?

Many say that the Old Ways died with na Imeacht na nIarlaí, the Flight of the Earls.

On September 4, 1607, broken-hearted and defeated in battle, the last two great chieftains of the North, Aodh Mór Ó Néill and Rudhraighe Ó Domhnaill, left Ireland, never to return. In the century that followed, Oliver Cromwell and his men waged war against the men, women, and children of Ireland and the land itself, leaving devastation in their wake.

Uprisings came and went, often marked by romantic futility and a tilt toward martyrdom. If a man could not wed the land, he could at least die fighting for her and be buried in the same soil as the chieftains of old.

A century and a half later, the Great Hunger would claim a million lives as people fell down from starvation as they wandered from town to town searching for food. Whole families died huddled together in cottages suffering from raging fevers while the crops they had toiled to grow were shipped across the Irish sea.

In the wake of the Great Hunger, a new figure appeared: Caitlín Ní Uallacháin, na Sean-Bhean Bhocht. Cathleen Ni Houlihan, as she was known in English, was the spirit of Ireland embodied in the form of a poor old woman whose land had been stolen and who was forsaken by her sons. She was an iteration of the old sovereignty goddesses, and the songs and stories that spoke of her were an evolution of the 18th and 19th century tradition of aislinn poetry in which Irish men would express their love of the land in coded ballads that spoke of their vision of a beautiful woman. This poetic tradition was at once an iteration of the ancient love of the Sacral King for the land and a way to give voice to forbidden sentiments in a time when any expression of Irish patriotism was a crime punishable by death or "transportation" (exile, initially to the American colonies and later to Australia).

Repression and forced emigration had almost killed the language and culture but in my great-grandparents' time, a strange alliance formed between young Irish men and women who yearned for freedom and wealthy Anglo-Irish intellectuals who saw something that their own ancestors had lost centuries before still living on in the Gaeltachtaí, the rural communities where Gaelige was still spoken, where the old stories and songs lived on. The laments of Caitlín Ní Uallacháin pierced their hearts.

In 1902, William Butler Yeat's play, Cathleen Ni Houlihan, debuted at the Abbey theater in Dublin. The play portrayed an old woman coming to the home of a young man on the eve of his marriage. She spoke of how her land had been stolen and the man, Michael is deeply moved. In the distance, Michael hears the sounds of coming battle, as French soldiers come to the Irish to drive out the British troops. He runs to battle, never to return, never to be wed.

As the play ends, Michael's father, Peter, asks his younger son, Patrick:

"Did you see an old woman going down the path?"

Patrick replies: "I did not, but I saw a young girl, and she had the walk of a queen."

It is not a kiss but Michael's death and the seeping of his blood into the ground that restores Cathleen Ni Houlihan's youth and dignity.

In the audience at the Abbey Theatre that night was Pádraig Anraí Mac Piarais, Patrick Pearse, a young educational reformer who had started a school to teach young boys the Gaelige language and the tales of the great kings, chieftains, and heroes of old.

In the years that followed, Mac Piarais became obsessed with the idea that blood sacrifice could win Ireland her freedom. In 1915, he wrote "the old heart of the earth needed to be warmed by the red wine of the battlefield."

A year later, on Easter Monday, he led the boys and his fellow teachers into battle alongside some 400 other women and men of the Irish Volunteers, the Irish Republican Brotherhood, and the Irish Citizens Army. They took over the General Post Office, the center of communications for the occupying British forces. As leader of the military council that orchestrated the uprising, Mac Piarais was proclaimed President of the Provisional Republic of Ireland.

The rebels held out for the better part of a week while the British shelled the city. Dublin burned. At the end of the week, they surrendered. The leaders and many of the participants were sentenced to death by British military tribunals.

Mac Piarais was executed by a firing squad just after Beltaine. In the wake of the uprising, haunted by his role in having inspired its leaders, Yeats wrote:

> "We know their dream; enough
>
> To know they dreamed and are dead;
>
> And what if excess of love
>
> Bewildered them till they died?
>
> I write it out in a verse—

MacDonagh and MacBride

And Connolly and Pearse

Now and in time to be,

Wherever green is worn,

Are changed, changed utterly: A terrible beauty is born."[6]

Feeding blood to spirits is a dangerous business. Yes, sometimes they will answer the prayer that accompanies the sacrifice. But they remain thirsty for blood and keep demanding more. The way in which the prayer is answered will often be horrific.

So it was in Ireland. The martyrs of 1916 found others to follow in their footsteps. They fought the British to a standstill and the British agreed to leave all but the six counties that now constitute Northern Ireland. The agreement divided the rebels and led to the civil war where two of my great-grandfather's cousins and another man where tied to a bridge and blown up by their former comrades in arms.

After the end of the civil war, an uneasy peace remained until a nonviolent civil rights movement in the North was met with brutality by British forces in 1968. Revived by the blood of new martyrs, Caitlín Ní Uallacháin called to a new generation of rebels to take up arms in Her name again. The Irish diaspora in Boston and New York became involved in smuggling guns and money to the Provisional Irish Republican Army.

Sixty-five years and two days after Mac Piarais was executed, another of Caitlín Ní Uallacháin's lovers, the poet and

6. Green is, of course, the national color of Ireland. But Yeats, who wrote many books about Irish folklore, would have also known that it was a color favored by the Daoine Sidhe who sleep beneath the Hollow Hills.

revolutionary Roibeárd Gearóid Ó Seachnasaigh, known in English as Bobby Sands, died due to a hunger strike protesting the torture visited on him and his fellow prisoners of war. In the wake of his death, resistance to British rule became more brutal and desperate. More and more civilians were killed by both sides in the conflict known as "The Troubles." The bloodshed continued until Good Friday of 1988.

It resumed in 2019 when the police launched house to house raids in the neighborhood of Derry where Ó Seachnasaigh had lived in the days leading up to the anniversary of the Easter Uprising. Dissident rebels who believed Brexit rendered the Good Friday Agreement null and void opened fire on police. They accidentally shot and killed a young journalist, Lyra McKee.

McKee's death shocked the nation and seemed at last to break the spell and bring an end to the blood sacrifice—for now, at least.

Reflecting on her death, I remember the words of Victor Anderson:

> "If innocent blood be shed by evil priests in wrongful sacrifice, the Gods will honor it even as the earth honors it and brings forth vegetation nourished by innocent blood."

What, then takes the place of that terrible sacrifice, as the earth tries again to bring forth vegetation?

Depression, suicide, and alcohol take the place of revolution in the lives of men who would have been warriors in another time. Too often that violence spills over into the lives of everyone around them. Victor Anderson warned that if humankind does not choose to move forward with intelligence and hard-won wisdom, it would once again be fated to degrade. We would slide back to the times of ages past where sacrifice returns with a vengeance and almost all of life would exist in the hell of its own making. What a terrifying sorrow that would be.

When the land is not fed life, it withers. Given enough dry seasons, it will ask for blood instead. While blazing heat dries Ireland for a second year, a generation that has redefined warriorship through its fights to re-establish the rights to birth control, divorce, and same sex marriage that were taken from the Irish a thousand years ago, now joins the struggle to avert climate disaster through cultural, political, and economic transformation. Many in the diaspora have joined that fight as well.

What happens if instead of going to battle in Caitlín Ní Uallacháin's name, we meet Her with love? If instead of dying for the land, we again offer to live for it, reclaiming our Sovereignty again. If we remember that we are Kings, will She remember that She is the one who brings the flowers of May and the snows of winter?

Turn to kiss her.

"The price of this kiss is your life."

Poems

Beloved

The darkness
beheld Herself
in the curved mirror
of time and space

and fell in love
and in lust
with Her own
reflection.

The exhalation
of Her ecstasy
condensed into matter,
becoming stars
that were born and died
again and again

and from their bodies,
She drew forth my own,
and said,
"You are my Beloved."

But I said to Her

"How can these arms
hold all the galaxies?

"How can this heart

hold your immensity?

"How can I drink in
the infinite river
of your wetness
and not drown?"

So, She showed me
a glimmer
of you
in Her dark mirror

and I searched for you
in the lithe limbs
of the Beech

I tasted you
in honey and salt and soil

I felt you
in the tides
and the storm
and the stillness

and I sent for you
with Sweetgrass smoke

I called your name
to the night

I stood before the Hawthorn
with offerings of whiskey

and my full moon seed

calling the Wild Queen
to bring you to me

and when I found you
in the sweltering smoky summer

you met my eyes
and then gazed into
dark water.
When my own gaze
followed yours,

I saw my root
in the root of Oak,

I heard my cries of ecstasy
in the elk's bugling
and the lone wolf's howl
and the songs of whales,

I tasted Devil's Club and Osha
on my skin,

and, at last,
I let her stars shine on me
revealing
my reflection

ready to meet you.

Ambrán Anama

All that I am was forged in the fire
at the center of the universe
and I carry also that flame.

I have been a great whale
swimming in the oceans
between stars
carrying the seeds of life
on my back

and I have been the one
whose song called
forth forests
growing in my footsteps.

I have been the sun
touching all the world
with my bright and fiery lust

and I have been an ocean
crashing on rocky cliffs

and the water that carves out
a cave at the roots of a mountain
and the hermit who lived in that cave

and the black serpent
coiled at the bottom
of the well below.

I was the poet who sang
the song that made the old gods fall

and I was also their prince.

I was the one cast into the waters to drown
and I was the one made lord of worlds beneath them
and I made the black mountain rise again
before the flood receded.

I stood on its cliffs
and called forth my lover
from the waves

and together we buried my heart
beneath a stone cairn
wrapped in seal skin

before Her world disappeared.

I have slept 10,000 years
and I will sleep no more.

I am the shatterer of pavement
and I am the songkeeper of the world beneath it
rousing those whose bones have turned to dust.

I speak with tongues of fire
that can set passions blazing
or burn illusion into diamond clarity.

Asleep beneath the ground
I learned the root song
that makes us whole again

and if you come close
I will whisper it in your ear.

I am a god—
creator of worlds.

I am that I am
and all that I ever was.

The Road to Dún Aonghasa

The dolphin rises,
guiding the ferry
toward Inis Mór
pulling into the quay,
the captain leans in
and tells you
"History on this island
has layers
The waterman has
always had a connection
with the underworld
Perhaps at
Dún Aonghasa
you will begin
to understand."

ii.

The road to
Dún Aonghasa
begins at Kilronan --
"Church of the Seal"
The god of love
insists you approach
not on your knees

but your feet,
their soles kissing
the body
of his Beloved.

iii.

Your first task
is to understand
that the distinction
between Pagan
and Christian
means nothing here.
The only altars
worthy of him
are the altar of your body
and the body of the world.
The first ones
called saints
did not preach,
they listened.
Across the bay,
four centuries
before Strongbow,
a thousand years
before Cromwell,
Colman c Duagh
spent seven years
praying in a cave,
speaking with mice,
drinking the waters
that rose from rocks
surrounded by Oaks.

The Oaks are gone now,
felled by invaders' axes
to build frigates
and slave ships
and galleons
but at the mouth of his cave
the Hazels return,
and among them
a fire again began to blaze
in your head,
sending you
over the water
to walk the road
to Dún Aonghasa.

iv.

Macha is the first
to meet you
along the road
standing over
a foal you thought
was stillborn
until you lay
Angelica and Honeysuckle
on the stone wall
and watch him stir.

v.

I will not tell you
the words on the sign
that point you

toward the old church,
they are the local name
for the servant of the one
the god of love loves,
and he will not see you
until you have paid Her tribute.
You must climb over
the stone wall
and find the narrow path
through Hawthorn and Blackthorn
and Rose briars
carved by a Catholic priest
who climbed the hill every day
for a season
The trail winds
through bramble and bracken,
ferns taller than your head
you will be tempted
to turn back,
but if you are lost
the Blackbird and the Cuckoo
will guide you
to the foundation
of the teampla.
If the wind takes your offerings
before you have arranged them properly
than you may proceed
to her well,
anointing
head and heart
and sex
with her wild waters,
submitting to

the true baptism
of desire.

vi.

She will not want
to let you go,
brambles will grab you
as you descend
until you proclaim yourself
her wild lover ...
and then the metal gate
will open but refuse to close
as you continue
on the road
to Dún Aonghasa.

vii.

He appears now
in the form of a heron
leading you along the rim
of the bowl of tears
the fortress
of his heart
rising dark
on the horizon.
Nettle seeds sustain you
as you climb the hill
that was an ancient seabed
past sharp standing stones
beyond the rock wall

where you lay
Roses and Red Clover
on his altar...

viii.

And finally,
on cliffs that tumble
toward the Atlantic he reveals to you
his secret:
if love is a prayer
and desire a gift,

    they are the driftwood
    and peat
from which you build
the needfire
on the highest peak
not knowing
if it will guide
the Beloved's curragh
home from stormy seas
or be just another light
amid the stars
that lead her
onward into mystery.

Origins

The Red Deer told me
that life began
when lighting
struck water
and stone
and set them
into motion,
so I asked
the Oak
to teach me
to root
in the earth
and draw
sparks of life
down
from the storm clouds
to waken the ones
who sleep
beneath the hollow hills
that the world
might bloom again.

Freya's Tears

I wondered
why the one Spruce
was so generous
with her resin today,
Golden like Freya's tears,

Then I saw that it flowed
from the place
where the Woodpecker
had been drumming,

and I knew
it was all one prayer.

Winter Queen

Mo Bhanríon Fiáin
comes riding
the Black North Wind,

leaving tracks
in the snow
by starlight.

drawing
as close
as my breath.

Tasting
of honey
and spices,

she kisses me
like the darkness
kisses the hills,

and all
my lips
and tongue
shall do
forevermore

is sing her praises
in songs that sink
deep into the earth

where they shape
the dreams of
deep roots

and sleeping seeds
that the forest
might live again.

Respite

Drunk on the scent of apple blossoms,
and half forgetting my name
I stumble toward your doorstep
following a song on the wind.

Cailleach but not crone,
you stand this side of the gate
where Trillium blooms white and pink
and turns toward the sun.

You fill my bowl
from a pot of simmering bones,
and I drink deep

as you watch
with eyes
that take me in
without betraying
what they see:

a wounded, weary wanderer
or a once and future King.

But when night comes
I hold you close,
In the space where worlds begin and end.

Scorpio Rising

Maybe it's the Scorpio rising
that makes the scent
of sex and death cling to my skin
when I slip between worlds,

reminding you of when
I let my godself rain down
where Apples rotted
back into rich dark soil

watering seeds
broken open by the heat
of burning cities
and melting concrete.

Your body, never quite sure
what to do with the feeling stirred
when you catch my scent on the wind,

never sure what to do with darkness—
the last time you tasted it
it all ended in blood and fire,

but something in you hungers
for the searing blue
at the center of the flames.

And the crescent moon
you wear around your neck
was born from blackness
to which it cycles back,

but not before it shines
in silver fullness,

moving the waters in me
and calling down the rain.

Mac Tire

Let me tell to you
this secret:

Among the Red Deer
of Lough Léin
the name of the Wolf
is whispered,

held close to their hearts
as the name of their God:

Ancient one,
Earth's true son,

Who culls the herd
that the Oaks might live
and drop the mast
that feeds them
when the leaves have fallen
and forest and field
are barren as the Cailleach's
Womb in winter,

If not for Mac Tire
they would devour
branch and wood and root
until the soil
blew down
to the sea.

In the times
the wild Wolf came
he took only
what was given freely

by the ones
who tired
of their forms
and their names

and wished to know
the ways of
tooth and claw

and the song
he sings
to the moon.

Now that he is gone
they make shrines
of the hidden places
where the bones
of their ancestors
bear still his mark

and pray that he might
return to them
before fire takes again
the meadow and the bower.

This the Great Queen told me
Beneath the Oak

That lightning struck
Whose branch
She made
Her perch

Before she donned
Her cloak of feathers
And flew into
The falling night.

The Drowned King

There are those who say
you must never
pull a drowning man
from the sea.

When my lungs
fill with water
even though
I am on dry land,
sometimes
I wonder
if they are right.

But a silver branch
has washed ashore
covered
with white blossoms

and through the prism
of a drop of rain
glistening
in the sun

the waves

of the sea
become rolling hills
of Heather
and Gorse

and I set out
on the slate grey
path before me
not knowing
whether

I am walking
into
the dark
of the Sidhe

or calling
a forgotten world
back up
from the ocean floor,

or whether
they are
one and the same.

North Wind

Wolf wind,
wild wind

black wind
that blows
from the space
between stars,

sí gaoth,
gaoth dubh,
that carried
the shining ones
down from the North,

rattles my bones,
sets my heart
beating like a bodhrán,

stirring what sleeps
in the hollow of my chest
reminding me

I am rock and water
that has danced
through a thousand forms,

always returning,
always reborn,
always making my way
along the royal road to Tara
to make the silent stones
sing once more

An Dair

I am the Oak split by lightning,
that still stands strong,
roots watered by an Otherworld well,

and I am in the Yew in the graveyard
who hears the dreams of the sleepers below.

I am the Stag whose flesh has closed
around the arrowhead
in his haunches,

and I am on the blood on the Rose.

I am the one who beckons the storm
and I am the one who sings the trees to blossom.

Is mise fianna rí
Is mise rí dubh,
Is mise rí fiáin.

Song of the Silver Wheel

Arianrhod, Arianrod,
of the bright and silvery wheel,

I was bound to it
by silken threads
I wove of grief and fear,

I turned my Will
into a knife
and cut my own self free,

and now I dance
between the stars,

we weave and weave and weave.

Raven

Fiach Dubh,
a black debt
I paid

three months I hung
from the lightning tree

while your fierce beak
consumed me

and my flesh
became your feathers
and my flesh
became your wings

and in your body
I flew

circling high
circling high

until you landed
on my shoulder

and called me by my name

until you landed
on my shoulder

and called to her Her name
until you landed
on our shoulders
and called to us our name

and crowned with stars
she wrapped me
in a black feathered cloak

and I rose
and I danced
and I flew.

Winter Born

At the mouth of a river that mirrors the Milky Way, Ireland's first people built a stone chamber aligned to allow a single sunbeam to penetrate the darkness on the morning of the Winter Solstice, filling the chamber with light. Alongside the passage leading to the chamber, they buried their dead with beads carved from bone.

We cannot know (by ordinary means) precisely how these ancient people marked the Solstice. Likely, like other Indigenous people throughout the Northern hemisphere, they held vigil through the night, singing and praying until the sun returned.

We live now in a time of rising waters when the sun is obscured by the smoke of burning forests.

We stand vigil, uncertain if the sun will return.

We place lights on evergreen trees to bring brightness and the memories of life, marking a festival that carries echoes of the tales of a Winter-Born King, a bright light born of the darkest night, the harbinger of hope.

We stand vigil, not knowing what light will emerge from this darkness to guide us.

There have always been Kings. Anthropologists David Graber and Marshall Sahlins write:

> "Human societies are hierarchically encompassed —typically above, below, and on earth—in a cosmimopolity populated by beings of human attributes and metahuman powers who govern the people's fate. [...} There are kingly beings in heaven even where there are no chiefs on earth."

The great Feri Shaman Victor Anderson said that the sun is the god of this solar system. The sun is the center of gravity around which the Earth orbits. It arose from the great darkness and filled that darkness with light and heat.

The chieftain or the king is the center of gravity that holds together the community and the light that guides it.

The first kings were shamans who mediated between the human and the wild, the living and the dead, Earth and starry heaven. They wore animal skins and antlers. The dead buried at Newgrange likely included such chieftains.

Because the bodies of the Deer gave life to the people in winter, the chieftain who gave life to the people was the mirror image of the Stag. In the skies above, the constellation we now call Orion, shining bright in Midwinter, was his counterpart.

The Otherworld King of the Midwinter Sky led the Wild Hunt, the procession of the dead departing this world. The earthly King brought his people life and hope.

In the old stories, the King is wedded to the land, and his sovereignty is a gift the land bestows and withdraws at will. When the King acts with love and devotion to the land and the people, the land and the people thrive. When the King becomes corrupt or inept, the land becomes a Wasteland.

Civilization brought the corruption of Kings—the Sacred King who served the oracular function of speaking the Will of the living land and guiding the people into alignment with that Will was replaced by the monarch who imposed his personal will onto the land and the people.

In the West, the era of the monarch came to a bloody end with the execution of Louis XVI. In the collective imagination, sovereignty was transferred from the person of the King to the body politic of the nation-state. But true sovereignty had long ago been lost, when Kings ceased to be truly wedded to the land, and so the sovereignty claimed by the nation state was an empty one. The mob developed its own forms of authoritarianism just as brutal as that practiced by the monarch they beheaded, an authoritarianism whose mantle was taken up by the state.

Liberalism and libertarianism sought to reinvest sovereignty in the individual, a noble effort and intention but one which failed to recognize that true sovereignty can arise only in communion with the living world. They arose within a worldview born of the trauma of the violent displacement of people from the land they had tended in common. Theirs was and is the cult of the individual rational actor, severed from a relationship with ecologies, human and wild, insulated from the human and ecological consequences of their choices.

If there is hope to be found in this dark season of burning forests and rising seas, it is in the rebirth and reclaiming of true sovereignty, invested this time not in a monarch or a government or a corporation or in atomized individuals but in a new form of sovereign personhood born of wedding ourselves to the world and living our lives like Sacred Kings, as gifts to the land and the people.

The Irish animist philosopher, John Moriarty, said that the people dream the King onto the road to sovereignty. We have dreamed ourselves and each other onto the wrong road. But the night is not over and there is time to dream anew, to dream each other Winter-Born Sovereigns, who come in the darkest hour to restore the wasteland with our wild love.

When we step into true Sovereignty, the bright stars that we are shine brightly, illuminating the path.

May we dream each other onto the wild road home.

Further Reading

Anderson, Cora. *Fifty Years in the Feri Tradition*. Portland, OR.: Harpy Books, 2010.

Anderson, Victor H. *Thorns of the Blood Rose*. Portland, OR: Acorn Guild Pr, 2003.

Artisson, Robin. *An Caro Gwyn: Sorcery and the Ancient Fayerie Faith*. Bangor, ME: Black Malkin Press, 2018.

Benavidez, Cornelia, Victor H. Anderson, and Cora Anderson. Victor H. Anderson: *An American Shaman*. Stafford, England: Megalithica Books, 2017.

Benavidez, Cornelia. *Journey for a Tomorrow*. Megalithica Books, 2019.

Benavidez, Cornelia. *Transpiration: Poetry and Storytelling as Our Spiritual Portals*. Megalithica Books, 2018.

Buhner, Stephen Harrod. Earth Grief: *The Journey into and through Ecological Loss*. Boulder, CO: Raven Press, 2022.

Buhner, Stephen Harrod. *Plant Intelligence and the Imaginal Realm: Beyond the Doors of Perception into the Dreaming Earth*. Rochester, VT: Bear & Company, 2014.

Buhner, Stephen Harrod. *The Secret Teachings of Plants: The Intelligence of the Heart in the Direct Perception of Nature.* Rochester, VT: Bear & Co., 2004.

Ehrenreich, Barbara. *Dancing in the Streets: A History of Collective Joy.* London: Granta Books, 2008.

Glendinning, Chellis. "*My Name Is Chellis & I'm in Recovery from Western Civilization*". Gabriola Island, BC, Canada: New Catalyst Books, 2007.

Graeber, David, and Marshall Sahlins. *On Kings.* HAU Books, 2018.

Grey, Peter. *Apocalyptic Witchcraft.* London, England: Scarlet Imprint, 2013.

Hardin, Kiva Rose. *A Weedwife's Remedy: Folk Herbalism for the Hedgwise.* New Mexico: Plant Healer Press, 2019.

Kirkey, Jason. *The Salmon in the Spring: The Ecology of Celtic Spirituality.* San Francisco: Hiraeth Press, 2010.

Magan, Manchan. *Thirty-Two Words for Field. S.l.*: Gill Books, 2020.

Moriarty, John. *Dreamtime.* Dublin: Lilliput Press, 2009.

Moriarty, John. *Invoking Ireland = Ailiu Iath n-Herend.* Dublin, Ireland: Lilliput Press, 2006.

O'Donoghue, Rod. *Heroic Landscapes: Irish Myth and Legend.* Dublin: Londubh Books, 2011.

Reich, Wilhelm. *Ether, God, Devil and Cosmic Superimposition.* Farrar, Strauss & Girous, 1973.

Reich, Wilhelm. *The Function of the Orgasm: Sex-Economic Problems of Biological Energy / by Wilhelm Reich*; Translated from the German Manuscript by Theodore P. Wolfe. New York: Orgone Institute Press, 1942.

Reich, Wilhelm. *The Mass Psychology of Fascism:* Translated from the German Manuscript. New York: Orgone Inst. Press, 1946.

Richter, Michael. *Medieval Ireland: The Enduring Tradition.* Dublin: Gill & Macmillan, 2005.

Silberman, Steve. *NeuroTribes: The Legacy of Autism and the Future of Neurodiversity.* New York: Avery, an imprint of Penguin Random House, 2016.

Snyder, Gary. *The Practice of the Wild: Essays.* Berkeley, CA: Counterpoint, 2020.

Thompson, E. P. *Customs in Common.* Pontypool, Wales: Merlin Press, 2010.

Walker, Nick. *Neuroqueer Heresies: Notes on the Neurodiversity Paradigm, Autistic Empowerment, and Postnormal Possibilities.* Fort Worth, TX: Autonomous Press, 2021.

Wood, Matthew. *The Book of Herbal Wisdom: Using Plants as Medicine.* Berkeley, CA: North Atlantic Books, 1998.

Buíochas/ Gratitude

I am deeply grateful for those who made this book possible:

John Doyle and Cornelia Benavidez who spent countless hours lovingly poring over my manuscript, skillfully editing my words.

Cassandra, who helped shape an earlier version of the oldest parts of this book, and Rhyd Wildermuth who helped me bring this book into the world.

Victor Anderson, Cora Anderson, Gwydion Pendderwen, and all the Mothers and Fathers of the Craft, and my dear friend and teacher Cornelia who is my living connection to them.

Stephen Harrod Buhner who taught me to listen with my heart.

Saille and YP, who walked with me through the darkest times this book describes, and for my Beloved, the bright star who guides me home...

My ancestors and my descendants, and all my kin, human and wild...

go raibh maith agaibh

About

Seán Pádraig O'Donoghue is an herbalist, writer, and teacher, and an initiated Priest in two traditions. He lives in the mountains of Western Maine. Seán's approach to healing weaves together the insights of traditional Western herbalism and contemporary science. He regards physical, spiritual, and emotional healing as deeply intertwined.

Prior to becoming an herbalist, Seán was a political organizer in movements for peace, human rights, and global economic justice, and a freelance journalist documenting the human and ecological impacts of U.S. policies in Latin America. He grew up near Boston, a short distance from where his great-grandparents first landed when they arrived from Ireland. Since childhood, he has been an avid student of Irish history and folklore. He graduated from Dartmouth College in 1996 with a degree in English Literature and Creative Writing.

He is also the author of *The Forest Reminds Us Who We Are* published by North Atlantic Books in 2021.

Ritona Press is a non-profit publishing organisation advocating for plurality, tolerance,and respect for Pagan, Indigenous, and non-industrial ways of being in the world. Find our works at ABEAUTIFULRESISTANCE.ORG

CPSIA information can be obtained
at www.ICGtesting.com
Printed in the USA
BVHW030020090722
641728BV00016B/1744